Go out
AND BUILD
Your own
DOMINANT
TEAM!

What Commercial Real Estate
Industry and Business Leaders Say About

TEAMS BUILT TO DOMINATE

"*Teams Built to Dominate* not only shows you how to build a team of high performers, but more importantly, how to lead that team. This is your manual to success, if you wish to best serve your clients and grow your business."

—JOHN SANTORA
Chief Executive Officer of North America, Cushman & Wakefield

"Rod once again provides a curriculum of success regardless if you have a team today, or not. *Teams Built to Dominate* outlines specific strategies for enhancing your team's production."

—DYLAN TAYLOR
President and Chief Operating Officer, Colliers International

"Books worth reading should motivate, stimulate and ultimately educate the reader on how to enhance their personal performance. Teams Built to Dominate hits the nail on the head and provides a direct roadmap for success."

—FRED SCHMIDT
President and Chief Executive Officer, Coldwell Banker Commercial

"Collaboration is absolutely key to meeting the complex needs of clients today and in the future. Rod's focus on the dynamics of highly successful teams is right on target—don't be surprised if most of this book is full of notes when you are through."

—MARK ROSE
Chairman and Chief Executive Officer, Avison Young

"The days of the independent/solo practitioner are gone. With every great success, there is a great teammate or teammates. This book provides the manual for creating a high performing team, regardless of your market, firm affiliation or areas of service within the commercial real estate industry."

—JEFFREY RINKOV
President and Chief Executive Officer, Lee & Associates

"This book is the perfect follow up to Brokers Who DOMINATE. That book shared how to maximize your personal performance. Teams Built to Dominate details how to leverage a team for even stronger results and overall growth."

—KEVIN MAGGIACOMO
President and Chief Executive Officer, Sperry Van Ness

"An incredible book for sales team effectiveness! Teams Built to Dominate will show you how to review your team and position each team member for optimal performance."

—WARREN GRESHES
Author of The Best Damn Sales Book Ever:
16 Rock-Solid Rules for Achieving Sales Success

COMMERCIAL REAL ESTATE

TEAMS
BUILT TO
DOMINATE

ROD SANTOMASSIMO, CCIM

Commercial Real Estate TEAMS BUILT TO DOMINATE

Copyright © 2015 by Rod Santomassimo
Domus Publishing

To order additional copies of Teams Built to Dominate, visit www.creteams.com

Author: Rod Santomassimo
Book Design: DesignKrew (www.designKREW.com)
Book Cover Designers: FX Designs (www.fxdesigns.net)
Copy Editor: All My Best Business and Non-Fiction Copy Editing (www.allmybest.net)

Printed in the U.S.A.
First Published, 2015
ISBN: 978-0-9838349-1-5

This book is dedicated to all commercial real estate professionals who recognize the value of leveraging their strengths and the strengths of others for the benefit of their personal and their team member's growth and ultimately their clients' success.

ACKNOWLEDGMENTS

Like those profiled in this book, success would not be as possible, nor as enjoyable, without the collaboration of a great team. Additionally, consistent with the lessons shared in this book, my team has evolved from my family and friends to specialists. My father is my greatest mentor, but his highest and best use is not proofreading my work. My brother, Vincent, is my best friend, but he is far more valuable running our business development efforts at the Massimo Group than editing these pages. My mother and sister, Gia, are great supporters, and they are perfect, and appreciated, in these roles.

As with my first book, *Brokers Who Dominate*, I was able to rely on the editorial expertise of Lynette Smith, the layout and formatting mastery of Jessica Krewson, and the creative design of Anthony and Christina Tran. Once again, they transformed the manuscript into a readable and attractive product. Wally Bock, thank you for being my partner beyond the writing process. A special thanks to Ralph Spencer, who has been a personal consultant to me and colleague of the Massimo Group for many years. Everyone's participation in this project has added a tremendous value, not only to the experience, but more importantly to our readers. We make a dominant team in our own right.

I was more experienced this time around and knew this second book project would take at least 12 months to complete. I have been very fortunate to have internal experts at the Massimo Group whom

I can leverage and rely on to continue to operate the company so I can find time to write during day. Thank you, Maggie Chlebowski, our Director of Coaching, for making it your focus that our clients continually receive our very best efforts and maximize their return on their investment in themselves. And thank you, Helen Xia, for assisting with the internal administration and external marketing of this book project. Thank you to all the great Massimo Group Coaches for giving me the confidence that our clients are in great hands.

Lastly, there would have been no way for me complete this project without the loving support of my wife, Launa, and wonderful children, Giana and Nicolas (both of whom still can't believe people actually pay to read my books or hear me speak—thanks for keeping me grounded). Thank you for putting up with my long hours in the home office and time away from you when I was on speaking engagements. There is no greater team than the four of us.

CONTENTS

INTRODUCTION _____ 15

HARKOV-LEWIS _____ 29

CONDON-MCGREGOR _____ 45

NET LEASED INVESTMENT GROUP _____ 61

COMMCAP ADVISORS _____ 79

INVESTMENT SERVICES GROUP _____ 97

TEAM NELSON _____ 113

MASON RETAIL GROUP _____ 133

ASHLEY-HOLLIS _____ 145

WOSNACK-HARTUM _____ 163

SVN-MILLER _____ 177

COPPOLA-CHENEY _____ 195

CONCLUSION _____ 207

THE SCIENCE OF TEAMS _____ 219

READING LIST ON TEAMS _____ 255

ABOUT THE AUTHOR _____ 257

MORE INFORMATION _____ 259

TEAMS BUILT TO DOMINATE

Introduction

A lot has changed since I first came into the business more than 25 years ago. It was 1989, the year that the Berlin Wall came down. We had computers but no commercial Internet, no World Wide Web, no email, and no smartphones. They were all in the future. As you will soon learn, these developments in technology, along with other key industry trends, have proven to be the catalyst driving the evolution of teams in our industry.

But I am getting ahead of myself. It was exciting to be part of the journey from then until now as a broker, owner, manager, and executive for local, regional and national commercial real estate organizations. I learned a lot from the experience. In 2008, I founded the Massimo Group, North America's premier commercial real estate coaching and consulting firm. Our clients represent every national real estate firm and scores of regional and local firms and/or their individual professionals, managers and owners.

As president of the Massimo Group, my challenge is to help our clients identify and implement the very best of best and "next" practices in the business. That's why one of the first things I did after starting the firm was to study what top producers do to succeed so dramatically. That research resulted in my first book, *Brokers Who DOMINATE: 8 traits of top producers.*

Those eight traits are all important, but a few of them stood out from the rest. One was trait number seven: "Brokers who DOMINATE are team oriented." More and more I witnessed top professionals choosing to work in a team environment, and I wondered why certain teams were so much more successful than others. That question was the start of the research that culminated in the book you hold in your hand.

To understand why teaming is more important than ever and why many teams forming today are different from the "teams" of the past, it's important to review some of the profound changes in the industry over the past two decades. Here are six important shifts I identified.

1. ***There is more complexity than ever before.*** Complexity of business and regulation in general, both for commercial real estate and the entire business world, are a fact of life. Contracts, research, due diligence, marketing, client correspondence, etc., all require a greater level of attention and coordination than in the past.

2. ***Fulfillment has become more comprehensive.*** Deals are bigger, expectations are higher and fulfillment of the opportunity has become just as important and extensive as finding and winning the opportunity. As we will explore, in great detail, each of these essential phases—find, win, fulfill—requires a different set of talents and personalities.

3. ***There are more multi-location client opportunities today than ever before.*** These are highly desirable assignments. They offer the potential for stable and high-quality revenue; however, they demand a greater focus on maintenance. To succeed here, a team must be excellent at dealing with the meetings, client reporting and, yes, client hand-holding. Finding the business eventually evolves into servicing the account.

4. ***Access to information is greater now than ever before and will only continue to grow.*** With more information, clients can be more selective of their service provider. They have higher expectations and demand a greater level of service.

They expect this in all areas of the transaction process. They seek experts, specialists. Fortunately, this access to information allows the commercial real estate professional to secure an "expert" position more easily. However, you can truly specialize in only one or two stages of the transaction process.

5. ***Leveraging Skills in a team environment is vital.*** We all recognize leverage when it comes to real estate financing. However, more and more individual commercial real estate professionals are realizing the leverage advantage of working with others. There is still a significant segment of commercial real estate professionals who feel they must work independently, or in silos; for the most part, though, these are seasoned veterans. As we share with our coaching clients, just because you can do something faster or better than someone else, doesn't mean that doing it will make you wealthier. Leveraging the skills and strengths of others is your path to true success.

6. ***Collaboration is more common.*** More and more companies are implementing collaborative approaches and policies within their individual offices. The days of locking your desk so your co-worker doesn't steal your client information still exist, but they're fading and fading quickly. Will cooperation ever erase internal competition within an individual office of a reasonable size? No, most likely not. Competition, when structured correctly, is a healthy and productive format for profit. However within individual teams, collaboration and cooperation are key factors in securing a dominant market position.

Each of these six trends gives us fresh opportunities to serve our clients better. The seemingly natural evolution is to create teams with a portfolio of individual strengths and talents. As we will share with you in this book, dominant teams are much different than the teams of the past.

In my first book, B*rokers Who DOMINATE: 8 traits of top producers*, I examined why certain individual commercial real estate brokers are able to consistently achieve exceptional production. The eight key traits that I identified were represented by the acronym DOMINATE. In this book we will outline the characteristics of dominant teams. I promise—no acronyms this time around. However, for those of you who did not read my first book, I thought I would quickly review the individual 8 traits:

Disciplined
Oriented to the client
Market presence
Industry/geography focus
Navigate careers
Assertive
Team oriented
Entrepreneurial

Do dominant teams share some of these characteristics? Certainly they do. They are disciplined, oriented to the client, have great market presence, and are industry focused. They cover all the bases, even though some team members don't have the skills or personality of a classic top producer. That's a good thing.

Can you imagine if you had a team consisting solely of Bill Gates, Mark Cuban and Mark Zuckerberg? Sure, they can find and win business, but unless someone elects to perform due diligence and property tours—nothing is going to close! You may be saying to yourself, "I'm sure they would just outsource it." Here's the thing: Dominant teams don't outsource, and they generally don't have part-time team members.

So, if individual commercial real estate professionals who dominate have 8 traits, what are the common traits of dominant teams? Here is an overview of the five common themes we found with commercial real estate teams built to dominate:

1. Strong leadership
2. The right people

3. Communication to coordinate
4. Culture is king
5. Structured for success

Before we review those items in detail, we need to take a moment to specify what we mean by the word *team* in this book. Some people use "team" in a generic way to mean "the people who work for me." Some people use "team" as a positive adjective for a productive group. I've heard CEOs refer to their gigantic corporation as a team. In general, I'm using the classic definition of a business team: *A team is a small group of people making a coordinated effort to reach a common goal.*

Traditionally, we've seen two kinds of teams in commercial real estate. In the industry we've used the term for a temporary team made up of several producers and support staff who team up on a specific deal. When the deal is done, the "team" disbands. These are temporary project teams. I wanted to study teams built for the long haul. I call them operational teams.

That term could apply to a producer and his or her support staff. They usually include a senior (team leader), an admin, and other professionals. Even though team members may come and go, the team is expected to be more or less permanent.

The teams we profile in this book, teams built to dominate, go a little further. I call them *integrated teams,* a term I picked up from Craig Coppola of Lee & Associates. Integrated teams recognize that all of the key themes influence each other. Strong leadership, for example, sets the standards for everything else. The right people go a long way toward defining the great culture, and they work more effectively if there is communication and an effective structure.

Integrated teams make use of anything that will make the team more effective. They analyze the ways things like compensation, technology and meetings can make the team more effective or drag down productivity.

I created the following diagram to represent the way the different themes all influence each other. Keep it in mind as you read about the individual themes because the themes affect each other. And remember that every team we profiled is a unique team in a unique situation, so they may express the same themes in different ways.

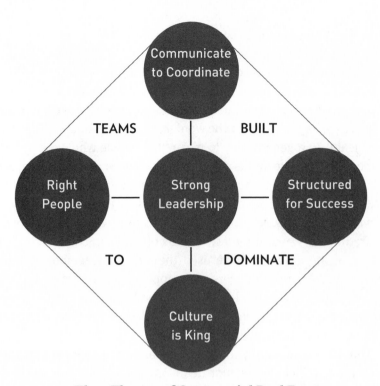

The 5 Themes of Commercial Real Estate
Teams Built to Dominate

Teams built to dominate have strong leadership. Great teams don't happen by accident. There must be a leader who creates the team and then makes sure there's a reason for them to stay together. Kevin Kohnen of the Mason Retail Group puts it this way when talking about his team leader, Jeff Mason:

> You have to have a great leader. If you don't respect that person and know that they are putting their absolute, 100% energy into it day in and day out, you're going to go somewhere else if you're good enough. I do think that to create a team, a bunch of leaders and smart men and women who can figure it out, you have got to have someone to follow who you are willing to go to battle with. I think that is the key. That is the absolute key.

In this book, you will learn how team leaders like Cathy Jones of Sun Commercial's Investment Services Group and Kyle Nagy of CommCap, a mortgage banker, use very different styles to provide strong leadership. You'll discover that many leaders have to let go of behaviors that used to work for them in order to lead a team effectively. James Nelson of Massey Knakal (recently acquired by Cushman & Wakefield) is a prime example.

There's one more important point about strong leadership. The leaders on teams built to dominate are committed to teaming. Notice I said "leaders." There can be multiple leaders on a team, or, more specifically, champions for each role within a team. They believe that an effective team is the best way to succeed both today and tomorrow. That means they look for ways for team members to work better *as a team*.

Teams built to dominate have the right people. In his business book classic, *Good to Great*, Jim Collins shared how you need to get the right people on the right seat on the bus before you decide where you're going. Dominant commercial real estate teams don't do it quite that way. They don't find generic "right people," put them on the bus and then figure out where to go. Instead they find specific kinds of right people because they know where the bus has to go.

The right people for commercial real estate teams have the knowledge, skills, and abilities to help the team achieve their commercial real estate goals. The right people also have the specific natural behaviors that will help them succeed in their role and complement other team members.

Beyond that, the teams in this book are structured so that team members have complementary skills. Sometimes team leaders add another team member with needed skills, like Parker Carroll did when he added Barry Forrest to his Coldwell Banker Commercial, Net Leased Investment Group. In other cases, brokers like Cory Wosnack and Mark Hartum of Avison Young join forces because they're specialists in different parts of the market. And in others, teams like Ken Ashley and Sam Hollis of Cushman & Wakefield bring on high-quality support staff, Whitney Hembree in their case, to help the team be more productive.

In addition to the right skills, the right people also have the right personalities. They must have a personality, or set of natural behaviors, that will make them successful in their role and be a good fit with other team members. At the Mason Retail Group, Pat West meshes perfectly with Jeff Mason and Kevin Kohnen.

The right people for a great team have the "right ambition." The right ambition is a team member's willingness to subordinate personal ambitions and success to the success of the team. Sometimes it's hard for top producers to learn to properly leverage their team, like it was for one of New York City's top brokers, James Nelson. But when they do, they learn they can be significantly more successful.

Because having the right people on board is so important and because a bad hire can ruin the chemistry of a successful team, the teams in this book are very careful about how they bring on new people. Some of them, like Ari Harkov and Warner Lewis of Halstead Property, have formal written processes, while others, like Kyle Nagy of CommCap, have a process that's less formal. Most use psychological instruments to gauge fit with the team and the job, but some do not. In the chapter on the Investment Services Group, you'll find out what Cathy Jones learned about hiring when she got it wrong, and how she's changed things.

Teams built to dominate communicate to coordinate. Coordinated effort is often the difference between good performance and great performance. Top teams use every available means of communication to help keep things moving forward and to keep everyone on the same page.

Team Nelson has a formal Team Operating Agreement that outlines the expectations for everyone on the team. Later in this book we will give you the access to a version of their Team Operating Agreement. Parker Carroll gets the expectations to his team through what he calls "metrics tracking," based on the principle that if team members do the right things every day, the team will be successful.

The teams in this book use technology to help people stay on top of what's going on. On most teams a CRM, or database, is the way this happens because everything is entered into the system and everyone also has access to it. But Wosnack-Hartum has a unique application of a common technology. They've developed an internal blog for their team members. Team members enter news and marketing information and other team members receive it on their smartphones.

We often hear how technology can separate people, but you'll find several teams in this book who use technology to bring people together. SVN-Miller, Investment Services Group and the Net Leased Investment Group all use technology to bring team members who are physically some distance away into full participation in their meetings.

Meetings are an important way that teams make sure people understand what's going on, how things are going, and what team members are doing. Most teams hold a weekly meeting at the same time every week. But the Mason Retail Group doesn't hold any regular review meetings, Wosnack-Hartum meets every 3 weeks, and Condon-McGregor meets twice a week. Harkov-Lewis has a daily stand-up meeting with every team member in addition to a regular weekly meeting.

Probably the most interesting communication medium isn't usually considered "communication" at all. I discovered that most teams arrange physical space to increase the odds that team members will overhear each other's conversations and will have informal conversations about business. Most of the time that means the team sits in some kind of bullpen, many of which are described in the profile chapters. Teams with private offices encourage open doors so they can overhear each other's conversations. And Wosnack-Hartum has a special meeting area, complete with whiteboard, so they can hold internal meetings where everyone can hear them.

Culture is king for teams built to dominate. Anthropologists define culture as "the range of phenomena that are transmitted through social learning in human societies." I like management thinker Marvin Bowers' definition better. He said that culture is "the way we do things around here." Every team we profiled in this book has a culture of hard work, accountability, and trust.

In commercial real estate teams, everyone has to have a strong work ethic. The top teams work really hard, and they expect every team member to pull their weight. Every team I studied was made up of hard-working people. But what that means varies from team to team. James Nelson starts his workday while he's still on the 5:50 a.m. train to New York City; and when he gets to the office, most of his team is usually there. On other teams, starting times and the time the workday ends vary with an individual's family situation. But everybody works hard.

Accountability and trust work together. When teams share how everyone is doing and how that affects operating results, it builds trust over time. This is important because for team members to give their commitment to the team, they must be sure that other team members are also putting the team above their personal goals.

Often trust building starts before the team officially forms. Bill Condon and Matt McGregor were friendly competitors when they decided to team up. Even so, they took time to work out the details of how their team would work. Getting it right from the beginning is important.

Often trust requires a leap of faith before a team can develop. When Sam Hollis and Ken Ashley first partnered up, Sam was the one with a book of business. He had to trust that partnering would make things better in the long run. Mark Hartum took an even bolder leap of faith. In order to join forces with Cory Wosnack, Mark had to walk away from national account business contracted with his previous firm.

Teams built to dominate are structured for success. I'm using structure in the sense of consciously organized. Great teams don't happen by accident.

Sometimes you make the team more efficient by adding a position. That's what Kyle Nagy did when he created the Director of Operations position to coordinate team effort. Great teams pay attention to developing friction-free work processes that help team members be more productive. They also pay attention to the social side of teaming.

Most of the teams have "team building" events that take them out of the office together. Some of those events are designed to give the team members an experience that helps them work better together. Team Nelson, for example, did one where they learned to row a racing shell. They've also done other, more social events.

Teams also develop rituals, little ways they can celebrate success or reinforce values. You'll read about Brent Miller and SVN-Miller's success bells, for example. But the most interesting way that top teams are structured for success is through compensation.

Top teams work to design compensation that values fulfillment, due diligence, client relationship maintenance and administrative support. That makes sense, given the major trends in the business at the beginning of this introduction. But the teams also work to develop compensation systems that that incentivize team success. Naturally, they do this in many different ways.

Some teams, like Coppola-Cheney, set the split for the partners a year in advance. For the next year they get the same split on every deal. The goal is to align their efforts with the interests of their clients and the overall success of the team. Matt McGregor and Bill Condon just split their revenue evenly. Other teams pay an origination bonus. Others pay a bonus based on community involvement. As with most of the themes in the book, different teams make different choices based on their unique situation.

WHAT TO LOOK FOR AS YOU READ

I believe that integrated teams are the way that most successful people in our business will work in the future. When will that be common? I don't know. I take the advice of the futurist Paul Saffo to "never mistake a clear view for a short distance." So, instead of making a prediction, let me suggest three kinds of ideas you can look for as you read.

You'll see things that are common to every successful operational team in every industry. All of them have strong processes that help them work more effectively and that provide social support for team members. All successful teams everywhere pay attention to hiring the right people and keeping them informed about how they and the team are doing.

You'll also see things are unique to commercial real estate teams.

Producers are still important, but they increasingly share the spotlight with important support functions. Watch for the ways that different teams make that shift.

If you want to dig into the research about what makes great teams, we've summarized it in a final chapter titled "The Science of Teams." You may want to read that chapter before you read any of the profiles. You'll learn what research applies to commercial real estate teams and what does not, as well as some details about what makes integrated commercial real estate teams successful today.

Finally, you'll see things that are unique to individual teams and that might be a good idea for you and your team. As you read, make a list of things you want to try.

HOW TO GET THE MOST OUT OF THIS BOOK

Use this book as a workbook. Why? In the 4 years since I wrote Brokers Who DOMINATE, readers have continually shared with me the lessons they took from that book and how they have applied these lessons.

Countless numbers of readers, teams and organizations used my first book as the basis of their weekly sales meetings. In some cases, all team members were asked to read a chapter and have a discussion of key lessons that week. In other cases, one team member each week was asked to read a chapter and present findings to the team.

There are less profiles in this book than my first, but each is much deeper. There are many lessons to be captured and, if you are willing, implemented. There are as many lessons in The Science of Teams chapter as there are in the rest of this book. Again, you may want to read that chapter first.

If you are reading a hard copy version of this book, make sure you have a highlighter and pen in hand. Abuse this book! Write notes, ideas, underline, star sentences and paragraphs—whatever you wish. Make it so much more valuable to you than to anyone else. This is your book. When others ask to borrow it, perhaps instead of saying "Sure," you'll think, "Wow, this is my playbook to my personal and/ or my team's success." Then you'll say, "Sorry, but I can't." You'll get the most from the book that way and, heck, I get to sell more books!

If you are reading this on an e reader, make sure you take full advantage of the notes and highlighting tools that are available on some of the more popular platforms. Also, in its digital form, the various links should take you right to the free downloads.

Speaking of downloads, whether you are reading this in its hardcopy form or on an e reader, we've provided many downloads that will help make this book even more valuable. You may be tempted to download them all at once. My suggestion is that you don't.

You won't get as much value out of each piece of content as you would by downloading one at a time, simultaneous with each chapter. By downloading the content that goes with the respective chapter, you will exponentially increase your learning experience. Plus, we'll be adding new resources from time to time, so you might miss the latest ones. Don't worry, these downloads aren't going anywhere. You will always have access to them. Just note, each download has its own unique password, which you will find in the associated chapter.

Finally, this is a business book. Yes it is structured on stories and people and their respective evolution of their teams, but this is a business book. As such, your goal should be to learn, evaluate, potentially experiment and ultimately implement those lessons that work best for you.

HOW THIS BOOK IS FORMATTED

All the team profiles are structured the same way. First I tell you how the team came together. The story form gives you a lot of information in a small space and will be especially helpful if you decide to form an integrated team. Following the story, each chapter has sections on things I found especially interesting and important about how the team works.

That part of the chapter includes details about how different teams handle compensation, meetings, splitting the work, finding, winning and fulfilling business and more. Mark the sections that interest you the most, so it'll be easy to review them later.

I asked everyone I interviewed for one piece of advice about forming a successful commercial real estate team. Their answers are at the end of the chapter about their team.

When you're ready, turn the page. It's time to start building your own dominant team.

HARKOV-LEWIS

Systems and Culture

Team Size: 6
Market: New York, New York
Focus: Residential Sales

I can just see your initial reaction right now. "What? A residential team—did I buy the right book?" Why in the heck would we start a book on dominant commercial real estate teams by profiling a residential team? Simple. The Harkov-Lewis team is not your ordinary residential team, and you can learn a lot from residential real estate and especially from this team. So, don't suffer from "That Won't Work for Us" disease. Learn what you can about good team practice from this very successful and interesting residential real estate team. Just this past year, Ari Harkov was ranked in "America's Best Real Estate Agents" by Real Trends/Wall Street Journal.

Many of our commercial real estate practices start in residential. Residential brokers were cooperating and sharing information long before that became common practice in commercial brokerage. In *Brokers Who DOMINATE*, I identified local market knowledge as something top commercial brokers use to dominate their market, something residential brokers have been doing for a long time. And personal brand building was common in residential brokerage long before we started seeing it in commercial brokerage.

Ari Harkov started out as an opera singer, and that was fun for a year or two. But the life of a professional opera singer is a grueling round of being away from home and living out of a suitcase. There's not much quality of life. So at 24, Ari decided he didn't want that life and decided to change careers. The question was: What to do next?

Ari has an art history degree from Vassar, so he hadn't picked up many marketable skills for the business arena. He wanted to be his own boss and not be tied down to a desk. He decided to get a real estate license and "see where it would go."

He tried rentals, but that wasn't for him, so he started cold-calling FSBOs. After a few months, things started rolling. He got some listings, which led to some buyers and then more listings and more buyers. He moved to Halstead Property and made his first sale in the spring of 2007.

Meantime, Warner Lewis was a successful but overwhelmed residential agent. In his first 3 years, Warner doubled his income every year. 2007 for him was a great year, but he found himself cancelling trips and other things he wanted to do. Looking back, Warner says that one of the problems was that he didn't have the systems in place to handle the business and still have a life.

Things got harder for everyone in 2008. Ari remembers having a deal set to close on the day that Lehman Brothers collapsed. That deal never closed, and neither did many others as business fell off a cliff. Warner remembers having his father come and "crash on my couch" to help him deal with the stress of real estate in the recession.

Warner had heard Ari speak at a Halstead event and he was impressed, so he knew about him before they met in 2009. Warner was going on a trip and he needed someone to help cover a big deal he had in the works. Warner took the suggestion of Halstead's head of sales and contacted Ari about it. Warner went on his trip, and Ari handled the details of the deal.

Both men immediately felt there was a real synergy. When their manager, Richard Grossman, suggested they get together, it made a lot of sense to both men.

They got along well because they had the same values and they were in about the same place in life. Ari had gotten married the year before, and Warner was newly engaged. They were both thinking about how to continue to increase their business success and also have some quality of life. Beyond that, they were and are very different.

Warner is a deal maker with a huge Rolodex file. He was putting on big events while still in his teens. He's great at finding and winning business. Ari is great at negotiating and fulfilling business. You can get some idea of their strengths from this example.

Warner has a friend who works at a hedge fund in New York. The fund likes to review information from unconventional sources, observers who are "on the ground" in a particular industry. The friend asked Warner to put together a short report every 3 months on how much real estate is being absorbed. Ari created the template for the report and developed a system for gathering the data efficiently.

Today the client coordinator pulls together the data and a collection of relevant articles. Then Warner writes the "color," giving perspective and insight.

This isn't a big piece of business, but it illustrates how the two men work together. Warner generated the business through his contacts. Ari created the systems that make it possible to deliver a helpful report every month.

Ari and Warner formed a partnership in August 2009. They weren't thinking of a team then. In fact, Ari still wasn't sure that real estate was the best choice for him. He started an Executive MBA at Columbia University with the goal of developing his business expertise and exploring possible career options.

Warner says he thinks Ari had "one foot out the door" during the time he was working on his MBA, but by the end of 2012, he'd come full circle. He told Warner he was ready for them to take it to the next level. Here's how he put it:

> It really seemed like the best opportunity to create wealth and quality of life and control your destiny, but without all the up-front exposure in the start-up world, was to build a real estate team.

It took about 2 months to organize their database and set up the basic systems to make the team work. In their pre-team era, Warner and Ari had hired a part-time buyer's agent. They brought her on full time. Next they hired an admin assistant.

Ari says it was their first true team hire, and it made a huge difference. It moved a lot of the paperwork and administrative work off Ari and Warner's desks. I've seen this with many of the people we coach at the Massimo Group. Hiring an admin assistant generates a huge jump in productivity and production.

Over the next few months they developed further systems. They modeled a detailed marketing calendar after one that one of Ari's friends used at a big bank. Then they expanded that into a full-blown marketing plan and budget. They also developed the basic manuals and forms and schedules they would use to run their business.

It took them about 6 months to develop the bulk of their technical, administrative, and operational systems. Then they spent another 6 months fine-tuning what they had developed.

Along the way, they brought more people on board. They've added two more buyers' agents and a marketing coordinator. In January 2013, they began working with a coach. Their coach plays an integral part in their business and with their team.

———————◆———————

Ari reached out to us for coaching, as he was referred to us by one of our New York–based commercial brokerage clients. I shared with Ari that we do not work with residential agents and referred him to Bob Corcoran. Bob and his team are top-notch residential coaches, and Ari credits much his team's success to Bob. For more information on Corcoran Consulting and Coaching, please visit **www.corcorancoaching.com**

———————◆———————

There's an important point here. It's common, and maybe natural, to see the forms and databases and meeting routines as separate items. Ari and Warner understand them as part of a business system, the way you conduct business. Ari phrases it this way:

> Systems and culture are at the heart of everything we do—who we hire, how we work with clients, the way we prospect for business, everything.

When Ari says that systems are important, he means that they think through and refine everything. Their basic process works like this.

Ari and Warner generally secure new business. With listings, they oversee communications with the seller, marketing, negotiations, and open houses. The agents on the team assist with showings with co-brokers.

With most buyers, Ari and Warner will win the business and conduct the initial meeting with the client and one of the buyer specialists, and then turn things over to their buyer specialists who take it from there with support and oversight from the principals. But that brief description doesn't give you the real flavor for how things work. A real life example is better.

Recently one of their marketing mailings generated a lead for a listing on a $1.5 million condo in Williamsburg, Brooklyn. Ari secured the listing, they assigned a buyer specialist to assist with showings, and they set up the first open house.

They consider an open house as more than an opportunity to sell the property they're showing. It's also a great opportunity to find new business. So at least one of the principals will usually attend an open house for that purpose. At this open house, Ari met a couple who were looking to sell their current apartment and move to a larger home. He and the buyer specialist later met with the couple and secured the opportunity to represent them on both their sale and purchase. Ultimately the team was able to generate an additional $2.5 million in business from a lead on a $1.5 million property, which initially came out of a marketing mailing designed by Ari and executed by the marketing coordinator.

I recognize that "open houses," in the direct sense, are not a practice in commercial real estate. The point here is to ask yourself, "What am I doing to get in front of several qualified prospects at one time?"

One of the most impressive things about the Harkov-Lewis Team is the amount of attention they pay to getting the systems and processes right. What's more impressive is the way they've integrated systems and culture.

MEETINGS AND METRICS

If we use American business theorist Marvin Bower's classic definition, that culture is "The way we do things around here," then it makes sense to pay attention to the primary group activity for most teams: meetings. Ari and Warner have done just that by developing a meeting system that both creates and supports their culture.

Like many teams, they have a team meeting every Monday morning for between 15 and 30 minutes. Ari drafts the basic agenda for the meeting and then hands it off to the team member who will be hosting the meeting that week. This is an important part of their culture—empowering every team member.

Every week a different team member hosts the meeting. He or she will use Ari's agenda, but they can also add agenda items. There's also a "quotes" section where other team members can add things. The overall agenda may change, but one thing is on it every week: performance review.

The agenda includes the key performance metrics for every team member from the previous week. Everyone sees everyone else's performance and how their own performance compares to their goal and the performance of other team members. Transparency and accountability throughout the team!

The team also has what they call "huddles" every day. In most businesses, a "huddle" is a standup team meeting that's usually held at the beginning of the day to raise issues and coordinate performance. On the Harkov-Lewis team, a huddle is something a bit different.

Every morning Ari meets with every team member for 5 or 10 minutes. They review performance from the day before and the plan for the day. The idea is to master the morning and set up the day. Everyone identifies one "Eat the Frog" task every day.

Eat that Frog! is the title of a book by Brian Tracy and is based on the idea that there are some things in business and life that you really don't want to do, like eating a live frog. But if you eat a frog first thing in the morning, the rest of your day can only get better.

In business, a frog might be calling someone you're afraid to call. It might be just doing a task that you need to do, but hate. Whatever it is, the frog to be eaten goes right to the top of the list of things to do that day.

For a copy of the *Harkov-Lewis Daily Agent Huddle Checklist*, please visit **www.massimo-group.com/TeamBook**. Simply fill out this form, one time, to access all the download material offered in this book. I recommend bookmarking the subsequent team book resources page so you can quickly access future downloads. Note: you will need the password "Lewis" (with a capital L) to access this document.

Again, let me reiterate that you should not download all the material at once. Instead, download the material as you read each chapter. This will enhance your learning experience, and more importantly your implementation.

Touching base every day in the huddles makes sure that nothing gets too far out of whack before it gets caught. Ari and Warner also meet with every team member once a quarter for about 30 minutes. They talk about anything they or the team member think is important, in addition to reviewing performance from the prior quarter.

One key to making all this work is the ability to track key metrics for the business. Ari and Warner track everything that they think is important, including performance numbers and their deal pipeline, as well as the number of prospecting calls made, handwritten cards sent, meetings logged, and buyer appointments attended. That might lead you to think that Harkov-Lewis utilizes the newest and best technology. You'd be wrong.

The team uses the Top Producer CRM system, like many residential brokers. But most of the rest of the technology is pretty simple. It's mostly Word documents and Excel spreadsheets and Outlook. Their philosophy is simple—the best system for you and your team is the system you fully and intellectually use.

The technology is simple, and they use standard agendas and checklists to make sure things get done without much fuss or the need to think through standard processes every time. A good example is their "vacation protocol."

In the beginning, when someone went on vacation, it was up to them to determine and remember to do everything necessary for business to continue while they were gone. The result was that some things simply didn't get done, and people in the office had to scramble to handle the problem. So they created their "vacation protocol," which consists of two checklists. One covers the things that have to be done before a person leaves for vacation. The other covers the things they need to do when they return, like undoing the vacation message on the phone.

In addition to holding the other meetings, Ari and Warner also have a one-on-one weekly to touch base with each other and go over the numbers. They talk a lot about cultivating their team culture.

CULTIVATING CULTURE

Today, the Harkov-Lewis Team consists of Ari, Warner, three buyer specialists, a client care coordinator and a listing and marketing coordinator. All of the agents are on commission. The support staff is employed by an employment services company, following Halstead Property's policy.

All the team members sit in a bullpen where they can see each other. Ari and Warner believe that physical presence is important. Ari put it this way when I asked about any virtual team members:

> No team members are virtual. Some of our marketing and social media could be handled virtually, but we have found from experience that there is a significant difference in efficiency of use of time and quality of work when we can meet face to face with all team members and when we all work together in the same room. Even when a team member is out and working from home for a good reason, there is a drop-off in efficiency of communication and quality of work.

Obviously, Ari and Warner see physical presence as a key culture driver, along with the daily and weekly meetings. The team also has a mission statement and a statement of team core values that's part of the regular agenda for every weekly team meeting.

The other important thing about the mission and values statements is that their creation was a team effort. It's part of a strategy of empowerment and fits with other practices like giving team members the ability to add things to the weekly agenda. All of that is part of maintaining a strong culture where the behaviors match the values.

The daily huddles and quarterly review meetings help keep the culture strong by paying attention to the values as well as the numbers. They send the message that how you do things is as important as the results you get.

Like many other teams, the Harkov-Lewis Team has special team-building events. In their case it's a quarterly event that isn't real-estate related. Those have included lunches and dinners and volunteering at a soup kitchen. Ari and Warner also try to do small, personal things for team members, and every Monday team meeting starts off with a personal weekend activity summary from each team member.

Those are all things that reinforce culture. They're important. But one of the most important things you can do to create and maintain a vibrant culture is to hire well.

Harkov-Lewis Team Mission Statement

Our mission is to deliver premier service and results, exceed expectations, and develop lifelong client relationships built upon honesty, integrity, trust, and mutual respect.

Harkov-Lewis Team Core Values

1. Honesty and integrity above all else; long term focus.
2. Relational, not transactional; closing is the beginning of relationship and friendship.
3. No emotion added; calming and rational with fact-based decisions.
4. Exceed client expectations; go above and beyond.
5. Advisors, advocates, professionals with extensive knowledge and expertise; not salespeople.

6. Make the process of buying and selling positive, enjoyable, and fun.
7. Complete understanding of client needs: financial, lifestyle, and plans for future.
8. Treat all parties the way we would want to be treated: What goes around comes around.
9. Proactive, not reactive.
10. Constant and prompt communication; fast response time.

———————•———————

For a more detailed copy of the *Harkov-Lewis Mission Statement*, as well as a copy of their *Monday Meeting Agenda*, please visit **www.massimo-group.com/TeamBook.** You will need the password "Harkov" (with a capital H) to access this document.

———————•———————

HIRING TO FIT

By now you won't be surprised when I tell you that Ari and Warner have a detailed, formal hiring process that they follow rigorously. It starts with a detailed, four-page application that must be filled in by hand.

The application has two functions. It's a method of gathering detailed information about the candidate. And it's also a screening device.

Many people look at that application, consider the time required to fill it out, and decide that applying to join the Harkov-Lewis Team is just not worth it. That's fine because anyone who's not willing to fill in the application is probably a poor fit for the hard-working, frog-eating team culture.

If the information on the application looks good, the next step is a short, 15-minute interview with the client care coordinator. One purpose of the interview is to share information about the position and answer questions. Another purpose is to get a sense of the candidate and whether he or she would make good team member. If the answer is "Yes," the next step is a meeting between the candidate and Ari and Warner.

Candidates make it to the interview with the principals only if they have the right attitude and values. Skills are important, but Ari and Warner have found that they can teach skills. They can't teach attitude or values, so if the candidate doesn't show up with them, they're probably not a good hire.

At the meeting, Ari and Warner will describe the position, ask the candidate some questions, and answer any questions he or she has. If the candidate looks like a good addition at that point, there are a few more steps.

There will be a meeting with the candidate, Ari and Warner, and their manager at Halstead Property. A member of their coaching firm's staff will conduct a phone interview with the candidate.

The candidate will also take a personality assessment. Ari doesn't put much stock in the assessment because he thinks that what the assessment tells about the candidate is "too generic." Besides, the team's hiring process gives them a good sense of the candidate and how well they're likely to fit the team. I will debate Ari on this one; however, his perspective reinforces an essential part of the recruiting and screening process. Assessments should be evaluated, along with several other elements, when adding to your team.

TEAM ROLES

Ari Harkov: Principal (CEO) (Commission)
- Prospect for new customers
- Manage the operations of the team
- Oversee support staff and buyer specialists on team
- Attend pitches and bring in new listings
- Manage the team budget/finances/payroll
- Conduct team meetings
- Host open houses
- Host and attend seminars/presentations
- Show properties to select buyers
- Negotiate contracts for both buyers and sellers
- Direct marketing efforts and source new lead-generation avenues

Warner Lewis: Principal (Commission)
- Prospect for new customers
- Attend pitches and bring in new listings
- Host open houses
- Host and attend seminars/presentations
- Show properties for very select buyers
- Negotiate contracts for both buyers and sellers
- Support and back up CEO as needed

Porter Hovey: Buyer Specialist (Commission)
- Prospect for new customers
- Assist buyers from beginning to end of purchase —identify properties, schedule and accompany buyers to viewings, submit offers, provide advice to buyers regarding all aspects of the buying process, negotiate with listing brokers, etc.
- Assist principals with conducting showings for listings, hosting open houses
- Research market and stay current on inventory
- Conduct training—articles, videos, seminars, role playing
- Attend and participate in team meetings and track all client interactions

Ashley Clark: Buyer Specialist (Commission)
- Prospect for new customers
- Assist buyers from beginning to end of purchase—identify properties, schedule and accompany buyers to viewings, submit offers, provide advice to buyers regarding all aspects of the buying process, negotiate with listing brokers, etc.
- Assist principals with listings, hosting open houses, showings
- Research market and stay current on inventory
- Conduct training—articles, videos, seminars, role playing
- Attend and participate in team meetings and track all client interactions

Joy Jiang: Client Care Coordinator (Salary)
- Draft and coordinate execution of Listing and Agency Disclosure Agreements

- Coordinate listings of properties in database
- Prepare pitch books and other listing-related marketing material—postcards, brochures, etc.
- Obtain offering plans, amendments, financials, and completed questionnaires from managing agents
- Draft deal sheets and disseminate to all relevant parties
- Assist clients with board packages and coordinate delivery to building management
- Compile and submit closing bills and paperwork
- Compile reports for hedge funds
- Top Producer—maintain CRM database, track deals and follow up with principals
- Prepare and print Monday Meeting Agendas for team meeting
- Help two principals with calendar, email and showing appointments

Listing and Marketing Coordinator (Salary)
- Attend photography, floor plan, appraisal, contractor, architect appointments
- Manage social media platforms
- Prepare monthly newsletters and marketing reports
- Conduct market research for team and principals
- Maintain client databases
- Carry out additional projects and tasks for team

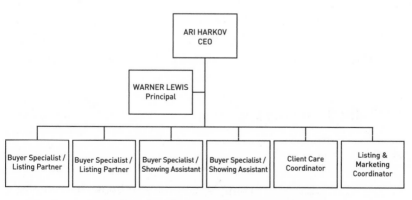

Harkov-Lewis organizational chart

DISCIPLINED ATTENTION TO THE IMPORTANT THINGS

You can learn a lot from this team. Let's start with the two partners.

Warner and Ari have a strong partnership and a strong team, despite the fact that they have very different work styles. Ari is a list maker and a planner who goes straight for what he wants. Warner is a contact maker and networker who may take a more roundabout route.

Many times people with differing styles spend their time trying to get the other person to do it their way, but these two men celebrate their different styles and spend their time and energy working toward common goals. They can do that because they have common values.

Both of them want to be successful in business and also to have a quality life. Both of them are committed to personal growth by stretching beyond their comfort zones. They've used those values as the foundation for a strong team culture.

They've identified the few things they think are critical to maintain their culture, and they pay careful attention to those. Virtual presence will not do: They want people in the office, so they can be part of the meetings and work planning and reviews that drive the culture. Ari and Warner are rigorous and disciplined about making sure their values are lived out in the team's culture.

In fact, they're rigorous and disciplined about everything. They use well-documented processes, checklists, forms and meetings to make sure things are done right every time. That frees up team members to think about the business and not spend time and mental energy figuring out how to do routine things. It provides a framework that lets good people do better work.

Any team in any business can learn from the way this team works.

IN THEIR OWN WORDS

Warner Lewis

I think the first thing is, you have to know yourself. That became crystal clear for me growing up. I played a lot of sports competitively. I was not a very good singles player, but I was a spectacularly good doubles player. I had a great serve and volley game, but being consistent from the baseline wasn't my game. And I ended up finding a partner who was a good fit. We won, I think, 70–80% of every tournament we got in because we just worked well together.

Knowing myself allowed me to maybe bend initially more than maybe Ari had to, [to] make this work because I saw long-term how this was going to make my life so much better. And I think I was not immediate-dollar focused. I was very long-term focused.

If I make X and I'm absolutely miserable, or I make X minus 10–20% and I'm happy, I'll take the second every time. Luckily, with our team, it's X plus ~400%. But initially, going into it, I just knew that if I had taken off my plate all the little things that I did not like doing, it would then make me happier and more productive. I knew I was never going to be a detail-oriented person naturally. And I know wholeheartedly that the two of us are an unbeatable team when it comes to real estate.

Ari Harkov

When all is said and done and everything sifts through the various filters, it all comes down to culture. At the end of the day life is about life, and it's about enjoying life. We love each other as a team. We love each other, we laugh, we have a great time, and we support each other.

There are days when someone has a lousy day or loses deals or vice versa or gets yelled at by a client or whatever. But ultimately we love and support each other, and we don't think of it as work. We're all excited to come in. We're excited to work with each other. Everybody's attitude is, "If you ask me to jump, I say, 'how high?'" No task is too small. And we work very, very, very hard, above anything else, I think, to build that culture, not just get the right people, but the right people with the right mindset.

I think it's pretty unique in our business. There are certainly teams out there who are blowing our numbers out of the water. And good for them. I know how difficult it is. But I think you'd be very hard pressed to find teams out there who enjoy their day to day as much as we do and enjoy working together as much as we all do. And for me, the culture is the number one killer for the teams, or the partnerships, that fall apart.

We have a set of core values, and we worked on that set of core values and mission statement as a team. Everyone contributed and everyone said, "I like this one," "I don't like this one," "Let's change this." We have that on our agenda every Monday morning, and we look at it every Monday morning.

That's the biggest difference between being a standalone agent or maybe a standalone with an assistant and being a team. A team with a strong culture gives you more. The 5, 6, 7 of us, we believe, are worth 10–14 because of our culture.

Ari Harkov and Werner Lewis came together almost by accident, but they've figured out that by forming a team they could each have more of what they want out of life and out of business. Once they decided to join forces, they put a lot of effort into defining the systems, processes and protocols that would make them successful. And they pay attention to all the little things that create the culture of the team.

NEXT UP

In our next chapter you'll read about a team formed by two top-performing commercial brokers who started out as competitors and became friends and teammates.

CONDON-MCGREGOR

Team of Rivals

Team Size: 3
Market: Seattle, Washington
Focus: Institutional Tenant and Landlord Representation

In *The Godfather, Part II*, Michael Corleone says that his father taught him to "keep your friends close and your enemies closer." That's good advice in commercial real estate where it suggests intensely knowing your competition. In the case of Bill Condon and Matt McGregor, it also suggests that your competition may be one of the best sources for building your team.

Bill Condon and Matt McGregor spent several years competing head on. That's how they learned about each other as brokers and as people. As a result, each one decided that other would be the perfect partner.

Bill Condon got into the business in 2003, straight out of college. He was married with a child and was moving houses on weekends to supplement his income while doing his runnership at Colliers. Matt took a very different route.

Matt struggled through school, as he was challenged with severe dyslexia. After graduating, he worked a variety of jobs, including ditch digging, roofing, fish processing and private detective work. On one job he got to go along on a sales call. That was all it took. He knew that sales was what he wanted to do.

Matt saturated himself with countless hours of training programs, including Zig Zigler, Tom Hopkins, and Brian Tracy, and logging thousands of hours of tapes and seminars. He put himself through the University of Washington, earning a BA in 4 years, and followed it up with a post-graduate year in commercial real estate, all while working fulltime. Soon thereafter, he began his commercial real estate career, first at Trammel Crow, then at Cushman & Wakefield. In the meantime, Bill's career was taking off.

Bill was a top-producing broker right from the start. He was National Rookie of the Year at Colliers, he's been among the top producers in the Pacific Northwest every year he has been in the business and he's been a Top Industrial Broker on the CoStar Group Power Brokers list seven times. He has been named on the Real Estate Forum's National 40 under 40 list on two different occasions, along with being on the Puget Sound Business Journal's 40 under 40 list. Bill is also a hard core runner, clocking between 70 and 75miles per week, running five or six full marathons per year and winning six of them to date.

Matt was named a SIOR/NAIOP Industrial Broker of the Year finalist multiple times and was recognized as the Broker of the Year in 2013. He has consistently been ranked as a Top Industrial Broker in the Puget Sound region by CoStar Group, and he was previously named Cushman & Wakefield's Top Five Western Region Producer. Matt has also won Cushman & Wakefield's Humanitarian of the Year award several times.

As they rose in their respective organizations, Bill and Matt found themselves competing day in, day out. They would constantly run into each other cold calling. They were both pursuing tenant representation opportunities and also representing several landlords. So they would bring deals to one another. Over time they developed a respect for each other, and then a friendship.

During Bill's first association with Colliers, he identified an administrator in the staff, Bethany Henderson, who was head and shoulders above the rest. She caught on to things quickly, delivered excellent work on time, and always went above and beyond the call of duty. Like Bill and Matt, Bethany has a strong work ethic and is passionate about doing the job right, whatever the job is.

In 2009, Bill left Colliers to join Grubb and Ellis (now Newmark

Grubb Knight Frank) as a player-coach, running their Seattle office. One of the first things he did was hire Bethany to work on his team. Bill knew how valuable she was, but so did Matt. Bill and Matt had become friends, but they were still competitors. Matt tried unsuccessfully to hire Bethany away from Bill. The real winner was Bethany, who used the situation to get a higher compensation package. All three still laugh about it.

While Matt was trying to recruit Bethany, Bill was trying to recruit Matt's entire team. Both men knew that they wanted to partner with the other. Bill describes his thinking this way:

> I definitely wanted to join forces. But as good as Matt was as a broker, what I really respected about him was the type of person that he was. In my mind, he was the only guy in the market I could partner up with because we were aligned on personal goals and business perspective.

It was just a matter of time before they worked things out. That time came when Matt suggested to Bill that he should change his offer to recruit Matt alone. When Bill agreed with that idea, they started working on details. Here's how Matt describes the process:

> Bill and I had some heart to hearts, and then I drew up a personal contract between us. It wasn't a legal document, but more of a personal contract on what I thought of him as a person, what I thought of us together, and what I thought the expectations were of us coming together. I described what I felt we needed to be able to do in order to take advantage of our talents. And I outlined an entire business plan, which he then redlined and edited back, and we batted it back and forth for a couple of weeks. When we were comfortable with it, we both signed it.

There was actually even more than that. Bill and Matt got their wives involved in the decision to the point of interviewing the person their spouse would partner with. Matt had his wife interview Bill and vice versa. The two couples spent time together.

Think about the process so far. Over the course of years, Bill and Matt learned about each other as brokers and as people. They developed respect for each other's work ethic, professional skills and individual strengths. They became personal friends. Even with that strong basis, they still took the time to talk through their objectives and hopes and expectations.

Once they had worked out their personal agreement, they did the legal paperwork, and Matt officially joined Bill and Bethany. In June 2011, the entire team moved back to Colliers, where they remain today.

One reason this partnership works is simple: It's a matter of trust. *Trust is one of the most essential elements of any successful team.* First and foremost, Bill and Matt are aligned with where they want to take their business. They both are very driven people who are never content. They push each other at all times to take their business to the next level.

The team does institutional landlord and large tenant work, along with industrial investment sales in the Seattle area. They also do national and international tenant representation. The partners spend 60% to 70% of their time on tenant representation. This work is both complex and comprehensive. It takes a great deal of orchestration, management and coordination.

Bill and Matt want to be interchangeable with clients. Although they complement each other with different personalities and skills, they work hard to make all their clients very comfortable dealing with either one.

To make that happen, they both know what's going on with every deal. Even though one of them is usually playing point with a particular client, the other person can step in and take over if necessary. You have to have trust to make interchangeability happen, but you need teamwork, process and technology, too.

Aside from the three core team members of Bill, Matt and Bethany, the team leverages other specialists on a contractor basis. They also use the support that Colliers provides. An attorney works with them directly at an advisory level to protect their client's interests, and works directly with many of their clients as well.

The team has a coach with whom they connect via phone weekly and at a couple of live strategy meetings a year. Many brokers think that only low producers need a coach, but coaches keep you sharp and growing, no matter how successful you are. That's why these ultra-successful commercial real estate practitioners have a business coach, as do many of their peers. Matt and Bill are not coaching clients of the Massimo Group, but I applaud them for investing in themselves and leveraging others to keep them sharp.

———————•———————

Unlike training, coaching provides a partner and a process that ultimately leads to higher quality opportunities and greater production. For information on our coaching programs, please visit **www.massimo-group.com/coaching**

———————•———————

It is important to understand that leveraging others, including outside sources, is an essential element of team growth. This team heavily depends on the Colliers Team Support staff, which provides them with a scalable solution as their business needs fluctuate.

The administrative staff supports the team on all project work processing needs, copy jobs, and deliveries. The marketing team oversees the marketing process for all financial and marketing brochures and mailers. They collaborate directly with the team on publication of all marketing materials. The research specialist gathers market research data and analytical reports from a variety of sources to meet any and all client needs, and additionally gathers research to enhance the marketing materials.

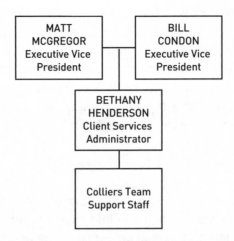

Condon-McGregor organizational chart

Another scalable team member is a "runner." Bill and Matt, like most successful commercial real estate professionals, started out as "runners," which also has be known as a "gofer," as in "go for" anything we ask you to do. They understand that the runner has responsibilities to them. He or she should call on segments that build the business and grow and develop in the process.

Matt and Bill have the responsibility to provide guidance and structure, so the runner benefits. That's why they set up an 18-month runnership contract that they'll extend to 24 months if the circumstances warrant. You can get a sense of how all that comes together when you read how Matt describes the runnership:

> I believe the runner's responsibilities to the team are to support us on efforts on cold calling segments we specifically design for them. Those are segments that are typically smaller deals that we're not calling on, but that we have substantial data on. We require a lot of cold calls.
>
> I don't believe in low-quality cold calls. I know there's a certain degree of success because of the volume of cold calls, and I also believe there's success because of strategy.
>
> I think you can only make 18–20 quality cold calls a day. So for a runner we bump that number up a little bit because

they're not going to be doing the same quality that Bill and I would do. So, with a runner, it's a little bit more volume. We want them to do 30 a day for their first year.

We also want them learning who the ownership groups are and where all the tenants are. We designed a flash-card system on knowing who owns the building and who the tenants are in any particular park. They need to master that for themselves and to make a contribution to the team. They'll also support us on listing work, doing tours, and things like that.

For their long-term career success, we try to push them to all the conferences. We try to get them to get their CCIM, get them to continue education, get them in front of clients, get them in front of prospective landlords who will get their name and their reputation out there. We try to get them in front of as many people as we can during that runnership.

The core team has had a lot of success, but they're already thinking about the next step. They're very much like the classic "founder's team" in the start-up world.

Most entrepreneurial start-ups begin with two or three or, at most, four key people. Those people work together for the first few years. Usually they develop into a tightly knit team, united by friendship and shared experience. But if they want to grow, they have to hire someone from outside. Here's how Matt understands the challenge:

As you grow in a business, there's a certain segment of the business that you don't pay attention to as much. You're not going to be cold calling on the 5–10K square foot guy anymore. A certain amount of material you've acquired in your database is virtually at a standstill because you're not calling on it. You're not utilizing it. And there's large revenue potential there. So you can bring somebody in on your team who can then focus in on some areas where you're not and capitalize on that.

Remember, it took the partnership they have now a long time to form. During the first several years, Matt and Bill competed with each other, developed a mutual respect and became friends. When they did decide to become partners, they developed a personal contract and involved their families in the decision process. They plan to apply a different process, but with the same kind of rigor, to bring a new junior broker on board.

That starts with looking for someone who appears to have the work ethic that Bill, Matt and Bethany have. There will be interviews with Bill, Matt and Bethany and with their business coach. Like many of the teams profiled in this book, they'll also ask the candidate to complete a psychological assessment. We will take an extensive look at one of these tools in The Science of Teams chapter.

It's clear that Bill, Matt, and Bethany want to do a good job of adding someone new to the team. They're committed to taking the time and working through a process that increases the odds for success. But it's worth remembering that this is one of the biggest challenges in any kind of business. Even with the best intentions and a good process, it may take more than one try to get it right.

DIVIDING THE WORK

This is a small team where everyone is involved in everything. That's necessary if they want to be interchangeable to their clients. But they still divide the work naturally, based on what each team member does well.

Matt McGregor is the planner, the person who's constantly thinking about the long term. He is strategic. Matt targets specific prospects and identifies the paths to business development. Bill's strengths are in connecting with people and building relationships. Bethany is the organizer, the person who coordinates the work.

The interesting thing is the way the team looks to an outside observer, compared to those inside the team. To someone looking in, Bethany looks like your standard issue administrative assistant. Her official title on the organization chart is "Customer Service Administrator." From inside the team, things look very different.

When Matt tells the story of defining roles as the team was forming, he says, "Bethany was going to be our team manager." Bill calls her the "team coordinator." Bill describes her contribution this way:

> She allows Matt and me to play offense, which is what we thrive at and what we need to be doing. She allows us to spend the majority of our time out in front of prospects, out in front of clients, where we need to be to get to a level that we want to get to. She continues to grow and take on more and more responsibility—more proposals, more marketing and ultimately freeing up more of our time.
>
> And quite frankly, she really truly does the work that it would normally take 3, 4, even 5 people to do. She's that efficient. She's that good. I can't stress this enough that she's a huge part of our team's success. I don't know, and I don't want to know, what our team would look like without her.

FINDING, WINNING, AND FULFILLING BUSINESS

Every team has a process for handling certain responsibilities in their business development pursuits and fulfillment of those pursuits. In commercial real estate brokerage, we call this the "Brokerage Continuum." This is the never ending cycle of Finding, Winning and Fulfilling Business. Here's how this team works that cycle.

Matt's the planner, and Bill says Matt is "as good at business development as anyone I've ever seen." That's why Matt is where many things start. Typically, Matt is the one who decides who the team should chase and why. He makes a list of targets and does the research and decides who to go after. Then he builds the plan of how to do it, whether it's technology, going out on a campaign, on a flight or whatever it is. Matt gets an idea of how things should go and then pitches it to Bill.

When Matt tells Bill who he thinks they should go after, he will lay out the technology he thinks they should use and the approach. Matt and Bill will review, evaluate and discuss, until they have it right. Then Matt will compile a list and get it to Bethany and say, for example, "Bethany, here's a list of the accounts we're interested in. This is what Bill and I have committed to doing every week."

Bethany organizes everything and manages it through the database. The team uses Salesforce with the APTO overlay. For example, let's say that the list consists of 100 targeted prospects. She will assign certain ones to Matt for certain reasons and certain ones to Bill for certain reasons. She'll look at the times they have blocked out for business development and she will organize calls during those times and prepare things for each of them. As I highlighted in my first book, Brokers Who DOMINATE, top producers consistently allocate time for business development. And more importantly, their team members support and reinforce this dedicated prospecting time.

If any particular research needs to be done before calls, Bethany will coordinate with the support staff and manage that process. Bethany makes sure the phone numbers and contact names and everything are in place for Bill and Matt to call.

When either Bill or Matt completes a call, they record it in their database so that anyone can find out whether they contacted the prospect or not and what the next step is. Bethany then organizes the calls for the following week, based on the status recorded for each.

They have a process in which, after a certain amount of time or calls, a team member can assign it to another team member. One example Matt provided is how to handle those who never respond:

> If I have been calling on ABC Company for 2 months and can never get a hold of the guy or the guy told me right where to go, I can make a decision about what to do with it. If I think it's a drop, meaning it's a waste of Bill's time for a particular reason, I can drop the account. Or I can assign it to Bill and let Bill know, "Why don't you try this guy? I didn't have luck with him for the following reason. I'm going to assign this to you." Bill can do the same with his clients.

Everything goes into the database. Everything. That way, any team member can see what's happening with any client and what the next step should be. Remember how Bill and Matt have created this position of consistency with their clients?

This kind of task process depends on three things. Technology makes it possible for any team member to find out what's going on with anything at any time. But that can only happen if everyone updates the technology so that it's always current. Trust is essential, and there needs to be a lot of both structured and unstructured communication, otherwise known as teamwork.

KEEPING EVERYONE ON THE SAME PAGE

Bethany, Bill and Matt work near each other, so there are lots of opportunities for asking a quick question or for a casual conversation. Bill and Matt are situated in private, exterior (against the outside wall) offices, with Bethany located in an internal cubical close to both. Bill and Matt say they have at least one scheduled meeting a day. They also have a series of regular meetings that set the cadence for the work week.

Early on Tuesday mornings, Matt, Bill and Bethany get together to review their listings and discuss anything important. Friday mornings they meet to review the week. If they have a runner, he or she is included in the Friday morning meeting. Bill and Matt usually get together for a lunch meeting on Friday.

I asked what a typical day looks like. Here's Matt's reply:

> On an average day, Bill gets up at 3:50. He answers any emails from the night before for about 10 minutes. Then he hits the road. He's a world class runner, and he runs about 10–20 miles a day and gets back to his house by 5:45. He helps get his family ready for the day. He's at the office by about 7:15.

I don't run 18 miles a day, but I do triathlons. So I have a workout and then get to the office around 6:00 a.m. So I'm about an hour in front of him. And then both of us coach our kids' sports teams, so depending on the season I would say that we are typically in the office until 5:00, 3 days a week, and probably 4:00, 2 days a week.

Most successful teams have a culture. I asked Matt about their culture:

> We are very hard working. We're all close. We're a lot alike, meaning the three of us are all very hard-working individuals who are all Type A achievers, and we all want to push the team and we all want to be #1. We're all three really good people. We trust one another 100%. There's no politics. There are no games. It's just three people who know each other well, trust each other well, have worked together and known each other for a long time and all have the goal of producing for our families and for our company and being the best at what we do. And that's all three of us.

It's easy to interpret Matt's comment to mean that everyone on the team should have the same personality. Having everyone on your team possess a great work ethic is ideal, but having all team members possess the same personality may not be. Teams built to dominate are made up of individuals with varying, complementary natural behaviors.

The team culture is reflected in their compensation structure. Bill and Matt share everything 50/50. It doesn't matter who originates the business. They know each other well enough, trust one another and are confident that each will provide more than their fair share to the team. Bethany is compensated with a salary and a bonus based on Bill and Matt's judgment. Everyone is aligned with the success of the team.

TECHNOLOGY AS AN ENABLER AND MULTIPLIER

Matt takes great pride in the way the team uses technology and says that they're "a leader in technology." It's tempting to think of technology leaders as the ones with the coolest, newest, and fanciest technology. But "coolest, newest, and fanciest" are moving targets.

The true test of whether or not a team is a technology leader is whether the team gets a competitive advantage from the way they use technology. Does the technology help them make more money than they would, doing business some other way? Does it help them achieve their goal of being interchangeable to clients?

This team's technology use starts in a very common place: a database. Everybody's got a database these days, but everybody's got a telephone, too. The test is how you use it.

Bethany is responsible for managing the team's database. She uses it to consolidate information, coordinate activities, and schedule. Every team member can log on and get the details of just about anything, but Bethany is the person who makes the database a power tool for building business and for keeping everyone up-to-date on everything.

Having everything online means that the team can be as paperless as possible. They use USB business cards, which include client video testimonials and live links.

The team also uses YouTube videos to market properties. If YouTube makes you think of kids with exotic costumes and shock-value makeup, think again. These are professionally produced videos. For a new property, the videos are updated to reflect the current property situation. For example, a large industrial building might have the marketing video updated to reflect "under construction," "nearing completion," and "ready for occupancy" stages.

The team tries to leverage technology for that key moment in our business: the presentation. There are always two big challenges. The first is to present what's different about your firm, to make the point about why a client should deal with you. The other challenge is to tailor your presentation to the client so that you answer the questions that are most important to them.

Here's Matt in action at a presentation. He shows up hauling something that the clients think is a big piece of luggage. It takes him about a minute and 40 seconds to unpack and set up the 27-inch touchscreen that he'll use for his presentation.

Working this way lets the team include lots of information about themselves and what makes them different from the competition. Here's the philosophy:

We know that there are other A+ brokers calling on the clients we call on. They're capable of doing these deals, just like we are. We all have great résumés. But who are you dealing with as a person, and are you going to like this person? The one thing we believe is people only do business with people they know, like and trust. So we try to portray that right away. We try to go there first.

The touchscreen technology lets the team store images and other details to tell the story of why the client will know, like and trust them. It also allows them to have the information at their fingertips that they think customers will value most. That starts with homework.

Research tells them about the people and firms they will be dealing with. They use a simple personality styles instrument to estimate what will work best. Here's how Matt describes the process:

Before I go into a meeting, if I can, I work to understand those traits and personality so we can adjust the pitch, presentation and introduction, whatever you want to call it, accordingly.

Then when we open up the 27-inch touch panel, we typically say, "Here's everything that we can present to you. You tell us what's most important. Typically we like to start with who we are, and from there, you tell us what's important."

We end up doing the same presentation. But we do it at their pace and they control it.

That's using technology wisely. The team analyzes the deal and the clients to prepare a presentation that is likely to be successful. They present things that differentiate them from the competition. And they modify the presentation on the fly, according to what the client wants. Technology doesn't change the challenges; it just makes meeting them faster, better and easier.

IN THEIR OWN WORDS

We asked Matt and Bill each to share one piece of advice about how to have a successful team.

Matt McGregor

You really need to take your time and evaluate the situation. When my wife and I got married, we had to go through classes and a whole process of thinking what marriage was about and evaluating whether we had the same values. I think more partnerships would last if the partners had to do something like that.

The big thing with Bill and me was I was able to watch Bill for 6–7 years before I joined him. And I really evaluated him as a partner about a year before I joined him, really thinking about it. And so there was a lot of process that went into that. It wasn't just, all of a sudden, you're joined in this team, in the job there, whatever the situation is.

I think taking time and really analyzing, does this person have the same goals that I do? Does this person believe and have the same work ethic and ethics in life and beliefs that I do? Are we friends? Because you're going to spend as much time with this person as you are, probably in actual hours of talking, maybe even more than your spouse, so you need to make sure this is a person you enjoy and that you know they enjoy you and that there's a trust.

Bill Condon

Number one is trust. I also think that you have to be aligned from a work ethic standpoint. You can't have one person who's working 55 hours a week and the other hour person who's working 30. That's just not going to work long term. And I think when you have a partner, you need to be engaged with them and understand their personal goals in addition to their business goals.

What really makes a great team is when you have a teammate who's pushing you not only from a business perspective but also from a personal perspective, and that teammate of yours is pushing you to become not only better as a professional, but a better person, and really wants to understand where you want to be 5 years from now, 10 years now.

Bill, Matt and Bethany dominate the industrial, institutional marketplace in the Seattle market. The one-time rivals have become the best of friends and teammates. Their personalities mesh in both their personal lives and their business pursuits. This particular team came together through experience. Bill first noticed Bethany's incredible pride in her work product during his time with Colliers, and both Bill and Matt witnessed each other's success by competing directly against one another.

Be careful in considering your competition your enemy. In fact, they may just be the best partner you will ever have.

NEXT UP

In our next chapter you'll read about a young broker who had the courage and savvy to bring on a more senior broker and then create a team that made the best use of everyone's strengths. It's one of only two teams in this book with a full-time virtual team member, and it may be a model for how other teams handle virtual members in the future.

NET LEASED INVESTMENT GROUP

Fast Start

Team Size: 4
Market: Austin, Texas
Focus: Triple Net—Commercial Real Estate Investments

Just 7 years ago, Parker Carroll was a Texas Tech student trying to figure out what to do after graduation. Today, he's managing director of the Austin office for Coldwell Banker Commercial, where he heads up the Net Leased Investment Group. He's also a CCIM and a top producer.

Parker has been in the top 2% of sales associates, nationally, with Coldwell Banker Commercial every year since 2010. Real Estate Forum named him one of "tomorrow's leaders." If you want to start that fast, it helps to have a boost. Parker's boost comes from his mentor, Rick Canup.

Parker and Rick met as a result of a job fair when Parker was getting ready to graduate from Texas Tech in 2007. Rick is CEO, owner, and principle broker of Coldwell Banker Rick Canup, Realtors headquartered in Lubbock, Texas.

For 2 years, Parker did general retail brokerage and leasing. Then something happened that changed his career path. He tells it this way:

> I stumbled into an investment transaction and from there fell in love with the investment side of commercial real estate.

> Helping investors accumulate and grow wealth through commercial real estate investments is an exciting industry to be involved in. I love the numbers, combined with the precision needed to negotiate transactions with lots of moving components.

Parker immediately started giving away all his leasing assignments and transitioning his business focus to single- and multi-tenant retail investment sales. By then, he had already benefitted from Rick Canup's mentorship.

The way Parker describes it, for his first 2 years in the business, he "sat under Rick's desk" and learned the business from his mentor. Great mentors set an example and also take the time to teach.

Rick sometimes took Parker on an appointment or let him listen in on a conference call. Afterward he'd take the important mentoring step of highlighting the lessons to be learned. Rick would explain why he did what he did and let Parker ask questions.

He encouraged Parker to pursue his CCIM and paid his way. In addition to lessons about how to be successful in commercial real estate, Rick used example and instruction to help Parker learn important truths. Rick stressed the importance of character. He also told Parker that commercial real estate is a great way to make a living, but you need to have a life outside of business, too. Parker would remember that lesson fairly soon.

In 2012, Rick and Parker partnered to set up the Net Leased Investment Group, and Parker moved to Austin to establish the group's office. One of the first things he did was to add Barry Forrest. Barry had founded Texas Net Lease in 2006 as a boutique brokerage group specializing in NNN investment properties to a national market. Bringing Barry on was a somewhat unconventional move, but it made good sense.

Parker had a clear idea of what he was looking for. He himself was 26 years old and thought he needed some "gray hair." Specifically, he wanted someone with a broad experience base and in-depth understanding of the net lease business. That way, Parker wouldn't get bogged down spending time training someone who was new to the business.

He had absorbed Rick's lesson about the importance of character and made that an important part of his evaluation process. Barry was exactly what Parker thought he needed. Here's how he explained it to me:

> He brought an insight to the developer mindset/perspective to our organization. Barry worked for several developers prior to launching Texas Net Lease. That understanding of how developers locate sites, negotiate leases, prepare for down markets, determine exit-strategy decisions, etc., is a great tool for your brokerage tool belt.

Younger brokers often hire other young brokers to work with them. Parker chose to hire an older and more experienced broker to work with, one who had specific experience in NNN investment properties. That immediately increased the Net Leased Investment Group's experience and contacts. There was another benefit too, but it wasn't apparent right away.

Parker is one of those brokers who track everything, including prospecting calls and email blasts and how many hours are spent prospecting. He reviews the numbers on a weekly, monthly, quarterly, and annual basis. That's how he noticed something interesting and very important.

Parker saw that he was making more money year over year, and that was good. But he noticed something that caught him off guard. He went back and looked at the figures again. He discovered that he was spending so much time in transaction management that he was not going out and generating new business. He was doing more work to generate fewer transactions and less new business.

That was on his mind when he attended the Coldwell Banker Commercial Global Conference and sat in on one of Ralph Spencer's presentations on teaming. *(Note: Ralph Spencer is a leading consultant and trainer in the commercial real estate industry. I am fortunate to have Ralph as a colleague and an adjunct member of the Massimo Group.)* Parker says that he had been thinking about creating a team, which was why he brought Barry on board. What Ralph's presentation did was to help Parker understand the difference between a team and a group of people.

The distinction is important. A team is a group of people working together to achieve a goal. It's more than just people working in the same office. I call that "working parallel." Each broker does his or her own thing, and they cooperate from time to time; but that's not a team.

Great teams are different from working parallel in two ways. Team members are selected based on complementary personalities, strengths, and skills. Team work is assigned based on the best combination of team members to achieve team goals. When those things happen, teams can produce results that far exceed the results of individual members simply added together.

Parker left the presentation with the goal of turning the Net Leased Investment Group into a true team. He understood that as a way to increase the production of the group and also a solution to his problem of spending too much time on transaction management and working more and more hours. He describes it this way:

> I knew in my heart something had to change. Handling every aspect of a transaction creates unnecessary stress and is certainly not an efficient use of my time and skills. I had to create a long term solution to elevate my business to the next level, while maintaining a great family life outside of work.

Bringing Barry on would deliver more benefits than simply adding experience and contacts. It would add that almost-magical feature of great teams: *fit*.

There are several measures of "fitness" when it comes to adding team members. We will explore the natural behavior side of "fitness" in great detail later in this book.

The best teams, in business or sports, aren't always the ones with the most talented players. Instead, they have talented players whose skills and personalities fit together. Then they can work as a true team. When that happens, both productivity and morale go way up.

Parker and Barry were individually productive when they were working parallel. They both did net lease investment sales. They helped each other with transactions. They bounced ideas off each other. That was good, but today things are different and better.

Today, Parker's primary role is business development and winning business for the team. Parker is responsible for day-to-day operations, strategic planning, business development, recruiting and broker/employee development. Barry is responsible for handling Parker's transactions once a property is under contract, from the due-diligence process through the closing. He also sources deals for himself and generates ideas for marketing, organizational procedures and efficiency improvements.

The two of them sat down and worked out the way they would delegate tasks in the transactional process. They figured out the best way for them to find, win and fulfill business. They made their decisions based on the fact that Parker is naturally "a business development and winning business person" and that Barry is a "business fulfillment person."

In the beginning, the team was just Parker and Barry. They "piggybacked" on the Lubbock office's admin support while they got their feet under them and got the business going. It wasn't long before that wasn't good enough.

Dominant teams of producers need solid admin support. At the Massimo Group, we tell our coaching clients to think constantly about their hourly rate. The hourly rate is based on your targeted earnings and the number of productive hours available. If you can pay someone else a lower rate to do a task, like transaction management or most administrative tasks, either hire someone to do it or outsource it, so you can spend your time on high-value activities.

Danyelle Quiroz was a member of the admin staff in Lubbock. She had expressed interest in moving to Austin. Parker and Rick had both worked with her and knew her work quality and strengths; they imagined that she would be a perfect solution to the admin problem. They also knew that she was a good fit with their culture and values.

Danyelle is responsible for design and implementation of the team's marketing platform. She handles the website, email blasts, LoopNet, offering memorandums and brokerage service proposals. She helps gather property information, aerials and photos and puts together marketing packages. With Danyelle on board, the team could concentrate on bringing in even more business.

In the first 7 months of 2014, the team did more transactions than in all of 2013. The surge in business created another challenge for Parker. Between the repeat business from existing clients, referral business, and the new business he was generating, the team had to start turning away business because there was simply too much to handle effectively. Incoming leads to the office were slipping through the cracks, and outbound lead generation began to decline.

That's a nice problem to have, but it's still a problem. In this case, Parker's mentor and partner, Rick Canup, was able to help come up with a solution.

Rick sat on the President's Advisory Board for Coldwell Banker Commercial Corporate, and one of the people he met there was Ethan Offenbecher, who was working for Coldwell Banker Commercial in the Seattle area. He was the kind of person who would be a good fit for NLIG, except that he was living in Seattle.

In his 13 years in the business, Ethan, like Parker, had been in the top 2% of sales associates for Coldwell Banker Commercial. Like Barry, he had founded and operated a successful boutique brokerage focused on NNN investments and medical office buildings. And like both of them, Ethan is a CCIM.

Ethan and his wife had thought about moving to Austin, so when Rick talked about what the team was doing in Austin and how they had uncovered so much opportunity, Ethan's ears perked up. Over several months, Ethan, Parker and Rick explored the possibilities. Ethan visited Austin several times with his wife and family. After working out the business and logistical details, Ethan Offenbecher became the latest member to join the team, coming on board in mid-2014.

His duties include developing new business, gathering due diligence materials, preparing marketing proposals, winning assignments and closing transactions. Roles include buyer representation, 1031 Exchange buyers/sellers, financial analysis and multi-tenant and single-tenant NNN retail and medical properties.

As of late last year, the team was on track for 30 transactions totaling $90 million. Despite the fact that the Net Leased Investment

Group is based in the relatively small Austin, Texas market, they've closed transactions in seven states.

They're just getting started. Parker is thinking about what's next and especially about how to add people to the team.

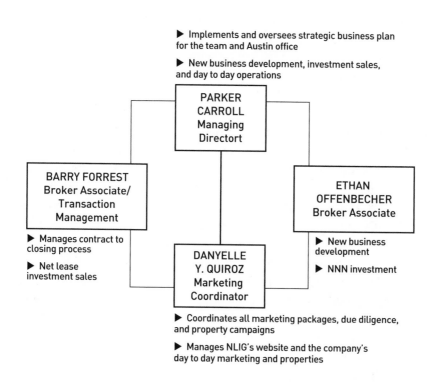

▶ Implements and oversees strategic business plan for the team and Austin office

▶ New business development, investment sales, and day to day operations

PARKER CARROLL
Managing Directort

BARRY FORREST
Broker Associate/ Transaction Management

▶ Manages contract to closing process

▶ Net lease investment sales

ETHAN OFFENBECHER
Broker Associate

▶ New business development

▶ NNN investment

DANYELLE Y. QUIROZ
Marketing Coordinator

▶ Coordinates all marketing packages, due diligence, and property campaigns

▶ Manages NLIG's website and the company's day to day marketing and properties

Net Leased Investment Group organizational chart

GETTING THE RIGHT PEOPLE

Silicon Valley entrepreneur Nolan Bushnell has said that "It's bad to confuse good luck with good management." Parker hasn't made that mistake.

He hired Barry before he realized the benefits of a true team and the importance of personality fit, as well has a good skill set. And he says that "Ethan was a blessing that just kind of came to us." But now he's thinking about a more formal process for adding new people to the team.

Parker has experienced the fact that it's hard to put "a Type B personality in a Type A slot." Everything and everybody suffers. And he's learned that in a winning team you need complementary skills and complementary personalities. Here's how he describes his thinking about process:

> Hiring the right personality type for the respective position is equally important as hiring the people themselves. I determine the position responsibilities and examine what natural personality type best suites the position I'm looking for. That would appear to be a common sense statement, but it's easy to overlook during the interview process, particularly if a candidate is strong in the interview.

If you've done any hiring, you know that's easier said than done. Identifying the skills and experience is usually fairly straightforward, but it's not necessarily an accurate appraisal of whether the person you hire will be successful. And people naturally tend to hire people with the same strengths and weaknesses they have, so some people have to do things they're not naturally good at.

For his next hire, Parker will be using the AVA instrument. We also use that instrument with our clients at the Massimo Group. The AVA instrument helps you make two key judgments.

First you can assess whether the person you're considering has the personality to succeed in the job you're hiring for. Top performing commercial brokers, for example, tend to have a profile that's similar to AVA's validated top producer profile. Top performing administrative assistants have profiles that are similar to each other. So do top performers in any role. That's helpful, because sometimes "experience" can lead you astray.

Harvard professor Boris Groysberg studied the idea that a top performer would be a top performer anywhere. Then he wrote a book titled *Chasing Stars: The Myth of Talent and the Portability of Performance*. His short answer was, "no." Sometimes a person has been a top performer because of the company or situation they're in. Their résumé may look good, but their performance on your team may not live up to it. Thus one's past success may or may not be an indication of future success on your team. It is key to ensure everyone is the "best fit" for the role and associated responsibilities.

Second, you also use the AVA instrument because it helps you assess whether a person has the personality to fit into your team and make it more effective. With AVA, you can also map the different team personalities so you can see at a glance whether you have what you need and whether the personalities complement each other.

Using a validated assessment as part of a formal hiring process will usually improve the quality of your hires and your team performance. Additionally, as we will expand upon throughout this book, assessments are but one of several criteria for determining "fit." And fit is only one success factor; you also must coordinate team members' efforts.

In *The Science of Teams* chapter at the end of this book, we will explore the application of the AVA tool in a variety of commercial real estate teams and explore how, when properly applied and interpreted, it can be a valuable tool for constructing dominant teams.

SETTING EXPECTATIONS AND TRACKING PERFORMANCE

Some teams in this book use a "Team Operating Agreement" to help team members understand what's expected of them and how that fits into accomplishing team goals. We will look at one example in the Team Nelson chapter. The NLIG doesn't use a team agreement, but Parker makes sure that everyone knows what he expects.

Rick Canup taught Parker how to understand his numbers. That's the way you know where you're good and where you need to improve. That's the way you know whether you're making progress on team and individual goals.

Parker calls it "metrics tracking." It's based on the assumption that if you do the money-generating activities every day, you'll be successful. Put another way, it's the belief that if everyone is doing the right things, then the business will take care of itself. Here are some of the things he tracks:

- Number of prospecting phone calls
- Number of prospecting hours per week
- Number of contacts
- Number of email blasts
- Number of presentations

Parker gathers those numbers every day, using a system they had custom designed for them. Here's how it works.

Every day, the system sends an email to every team member with questions about their activity. It takes a team member less than a minute to enter their activities for the day and send the information back. Then the system automatically consolidates the information into a report and sends it to Parker.

Perhaps you don't think tracking numbers is important. But how do you know you are winning if you don't keep score? Many CRE professionals create goals, which is a great first step; but then they simply progress throughout the year without monitoring their progress. Creating metrics that support your goals and tracking those metrics on a weekly basis has two critical outcomes: (a) By tracking numbers, each team member can be held accountable to him/herself and to the team; and (b) Having aggregated the data of our hundreds of coaching clients, we've discovered one undeniable fact: Those who track the most, make the most money. So do you still think tracking is unimportant?

Parker had the system developed independently, but it's a lot like the system we use with our coaching clients as part of our Massimobile platform.

———————

For more information on the Massimobile virtual coaching system, please visit **www.massimo-group.com/massimobile**

———————

SYSTEMS SUPPORT SUCCESS

Parker's system is an example of an effective technology-based performance tracking system. The best of those systems deliver on three dimensions.

The system doesn't depend on "remembering." Historically, activity-reporting systems depended on people remembering to send in their numbers. A technology-based system can send the request for information every day at the same time. That helps create a reporting habit.

The system is easy to use. People are more likely to do what you want them to do if you make it easy. Team members can open the email and send their information in less than a minute. The system can work with a mobile phone to make it even easier.

Reporting is automatic. The system consolidates the information and turns it into a helpful report. The report can highlight positive or negative variance that should get attention.

It's important to track performance for producers, but it's also important to track support staff performance. Parker doesn't use metrics to track Danyelle's performance.

Danyelle has checklists for the things that need to be done every week, like email blasts and updating listings and pictures. There's also a project-management component to her job. The team uses REA (a popular commercial real estate and CRM, or client relationship management system, or database) and uses it to track the project work she's responsible for. But before they get that far, the team has to find and win business.

MAKING THE CASH REGISTER RING

Parker thinks it's possible to have too much repeat business. The conventional wisdom is that repeat business is always good, but he thinks that in the NNN investment world, you have to pay attention to where the business is coming from.

Most of his repeat business is on the buyer side, so he concentrates his lead generation effort on sellers to fulfill buyer exchange needs. Part of the effort is tracking the ownership of properties and finding out who buys them and when they buy them.

Parker and Ethan primarily handle business development for the team. To handle the leads from existing clients and to generate new business, they spend part of every day on the phones.

9:00 a.m. to 11:00 a.m. Central Time works best for prospecting because they're dealing with properties all over the country. When they start, it's still mid-morning on the East Coast and people are still fresh. Prospecting follows the sun, so that at the end of their designated prospecting time they're calling prospects in California at 8:00 or 9:00. They've got a ritual for their calling time.

First, they shut email off. It can be a distraction when you're prospecting. Then they have what Parker calls an "open door policy." Doors stay open so they can hear and learn from each other's prospecting calls and sometimes jump in with a buyer or seller who's the perfect fit for the other person's prospect.

When they generate the opportunity to make a presentation, they pull together the materials they need. Then they may call on some of the people in the Lubbock office for a strategy session.

Parker says that almost all their presentations are virtual, since very few of their clients are located in the Austin area. GoToMeeting is their preferred platform for these virtual meetings.

When they win the assignment, the focus shifts to fulfilling the business. In the beginning they coordinated things with email, but success made that harder and harder. Parker looked up one day and realized that they had nine properties under contract and no system for making sure that everything got done.

Since they were already using REA, they asked the company for help in using that system to track all of the details. Now they have a system of reminders to let everyone know their responsibilities for every transaction. The person responsible for a task is also responsible for updating the system when it's complete. That's the technological side of staying on track.

STAYING ON TRACK WITH MEETINGS

Like most other effective teams, NLIG has a regular weekly meeting to bring everyone up to speed on what's happening. Actually, they have two meetings.

Every Wednesday from 8:00 to 9:00 a.m., they have their meeting. Most of the teams we studied for this book have their weekly meeting on Monday, so I asked Parker about that. He thinks Wednesday works better for them because they're each taking care of their "big rocks" on Monday and Tuesday.

So at 8:00 on Wednesday morning, NLIG has their meeting to coordinate activities. Then they participate in a meeting with the Lubbock office, using a platform called LifeSize as well as GotoMeeting when appropriate

This is another application of technology that we're seeing more and more. Teams are using high-quality video conferencing as a key tool to involve team members, no matter where they happen to be working.

During our group and one-on-one coaching calls at the Massimo Group, we rely on ZOOM. Tools such as Lifesize, ZOOM, GotoMeeting and other video meeting platforms provide a solution that is the next best thing to actually being there. For more information on our group and one-to-one coaching programs, please visit **www.massimo-group.com/coaching**

WHAT'S A VIRTUAL OFFICE?

I asked everyone I interviewed if they had anyone who worked "virtually." Parker's response was unique.

He said, "We are out of one office." In the next breath he said, "Barry lives in Dallas." I think both of those statements are accurate.

Barry is living in Dallas where he and his family have deep roots and where his wife works as a teacher. Parker says that Barry and his wife are considering a move to Austin, but it's not absolutely necessary for team effectiveness, even though it would help. Technology is part of the reason.

The REA platform lets the team coordinate their work on transactions without needing to be in the same place. Video conferencing lets Barry participate in meetings or presentations without the need to be physically present. But technology is only part of the reason why this teaming works across distance.

Barry also spends time in the Austin office every other week. That allows for the richness of in-person communication. It offers the chance for the kind of "opportunity conversation" that is far more likely when people are physically together.

In the future, this kind of "virtual" relationship may be common. Technology increasingly makes it easy for teams to coordinate their efforts and communicate effectively. When work processes are embedded in software, technology can actually make them more effective without the need for common physical presence.

But researchers tell us that, in addition to having strong processes and coordinating mechanisms, dominant business teams also provide mutual "social support" for team members. That's far less likely to happen when team members are separated by distance. Perhaps something like the way Barry's situation is handled will be the way more teams reap the benefits of working in a virtual environment with the strong social system that characterizes dominant teams.

Many of the self-help and motivational books would turn this into a story of Parker Carroll's success at a young age. But if all you get from this chapter is that some people who are very successful early in their career, you'll miss the most important thing. Yes, Parker has been successful, but he didn't do it alone.

Rick Canup gave him a big boost, right at the start. Rick hired him, helped him learn the business, and supported him with time, attention and money. He was also savvy enough to step back as Parker's abilities and interests developed. He remains Parker's mentor, but now they're partners in the Net Leased Investment Group, as well.

His team members are an engine of success, too. Teaming with Barry let him concentrate on what he does best while making Barry more productive at the same time. Danyelle provides solid support that allows Parker, Barry and Ethan to do more of what they do well and less of things that they don't like or aren't good at, or that they feel are just a poor use of their time.

All those people have helped Parker. They've helped him have a successful commercial real estate business. And they've helped make it possible for him to have a good family life outside of business, too.

IN HIS OWN WORDS

Parker Carroll

A great team is all about having the right people in the right position and providing them the necessary resources and environment to flourish in their career. In the words of Jim Collins, "get the right people on the right seat of the bus." A team firing on all cylinders is exciting and energetic. The enthusiasm that comes from each person's excelling to new career heights is contagious. On the flip side, there's nothing more frustrating, time consuming and energy draining than having the wrong team member or having the right team member in the wrong position. If you make a hiring mistake, fix it quickly. Do not let your team and office atmosphere suffer for 6 months or a year. It's better for everyone to move on and to do so quickly.

Be a team player. Processes and systems that work for an individual broker may not work for the team. But that's the point, right? Working together to achieve more than the individual ever could.

Be coachable. Learn from the top producers and top managers. They've walked in your shoes and made it. One of the interesting observations I've made throughout my career is that top producers/managers will share their ideas; you just have to ask.

For managers. As a manager, it's my job to unlock each team member's natural ability and elevate their performance to new levels. They have to do the work and be coachable, but we have to be selfless and be there to help, encourage, lead and motivate. You can't do this when your office door is closed 6 hours a day handling "critical" work. Schedule your time appropriately and give them the time and resources they need. Being a top producer and a manager has been one of the greatest business challenges of my career. However, if you plan to wear multiple "hats," you must implement systems to make you successful at both.

BONUS: RICK CANUP AND BEING A MENTOR

We talk a lot about mentoring in commercial real estate, and it's almost always from the perspective of the protégé. But preparing this chapter gave me the opportunity to see mentoring from the mentor's perspective. Rick Canup is obviously a very effective mentor.

In the chapter you can see how he worked as a mentor. He gave Parker learning opportunities. He took time to teach and to answer questions. And as Parker grew in confidence and competence, Rick was able to step back and become a friend, even as he remained Parker's mentor.

I asked Rick for some thoughts on mentoring and what he looks for in a mentoring relationship. What follows is his description of working with Parker. I think it will give you some ideas about what a mentor looks for.

Working with Parker has been a very enjoyable and rewarding experience for me. From his first day at the company, he has always been very teachable and moldable. He is like a sponge and eager to learn and actually implement those things he was learning. As we trained and he came in to see me and ask questions on how to handle a situation, he listened intently, processed the counsel, and then always did exactly what I suggested, immediately without any hesitation. That was most unusual!

To this day, he calls whenever more difficult or new problems arise that he has not previously encountered. We discuss them, and now he adds in his own experiences and has become a terrific problem solver for his clients and the office.

Over my 67 years, I have come to realize that the most important quality I am looking for in an associate, staff member or a close friend is character. Parker is a man of character. I feel and think of Parker as one of my own grandsons, and we have grown very close over these last 7 years. We have a very special relationship, and I trust him implicitly.

There are many places in commercial real estate where people use the word "team" to mean people who are just working for the same group. As I mentioned in an earlier chapter, I call that "working in parallel." Parker Carroll is one of the team leaders in this book who made a conscious effort to move beyond that by dividing the work so that team members do more of the things that they're good at. It's worked for him, and it should work for you, too.

NEXT UP

The team leader in the next chapter stands out from most of the others in this book. He would think that's fine because he consciously tries to do things differently and better. The results include some unique policies and practices that should give you some good ideas.

COMMCAP ADVISORS

Normal Sucks!

Team Size: 5
Markets: Las Vegas, Nevada
Focus: Commercial Real Estate Mortgage Banking

Teams evolve over time. However, they don't happen automatically. It takes someone with the desire to create a team who is willing to take the action to make it happen. Many times we learn from teams we have been part of, prior to building our own teams. We learn from our prior experience, but ultimately put our own mark on what the team will become and how it will be perceived in the market.

This was the case of Kyle Nagy. Kyle would make Horatio Alger proud. Alger was the 19th century American author who wrote dozens of books about young men who pulled themselves from modest means to success by "pluck and luck."

Kyle's story starts in Merrillville, Indiana, just a little south of Gary. As Kyle say:

> You can Google Gary and find the crime rates, homicides and all the fun stats. Although my mother did go to college when I was in high school, my upbringing was not in a professional environment. There were no doctors, lawyers, accountants or teachers in my neighborhood.

In 1994 he headed west to college, first at the College of Southern Nevada and then at the University of Nevada, Las Vegas (UNLV). Kyle says he wasn't much of a student in high school, but he applied himself in college and made the Dean's List every semester at UNLV on his way to earning a Bachelor of Science in Business Administration in economics. When he was getting ready to graduate in 1999, he went looking for a job.

At that point in his life, Kyle wasn't sure what he wanted to do, but he thought he knew where he wanted to work. He went to the Hughes Center. Here's his description of why:

> During my final year of college, my econ professors would mention Hughes Center when referencing successful professionals. It was our only true Class A office park at the time. The top national and regional companies had offices there. It was the central business district and financial center. It was where wealth was made and where wealth worked.

The interview that opened his eyes was for a life insurance sales position. The interviewer described how they were going to build his book of business from the people he knew. That was going to be a problem. Kyle didn't come from a connected family, and all his friends from college were "broke and playing ice hockey." He didn't know anyone he could use to build a book of business.

It was one of those meetings that make you feel like you're only as valuable as what people can take from you. So Kyle took the résumés he brought with him, with the objective of working anywhere in this office complex, and he started knocking on doors.

Behind one of those doors were Keith and Patti Russell. While they were sitting at their table, having lunch, Kyle gave them his pitch which basically was telling them his name, handing them his résumé, and telling them he was about to graduate from UNLV. Two weeks later, Keith called him and asked what he knew about apartment buildings and shopping centers.

Kyle told him, "I live in an apartment building, and my fiancée likes to shop." Looking back, Kyle realized that it was probably not the best answer to give someone who's working in commercial real estate, but it worked for him.

Keith probably figured that since Kyle, at 22–23 years old, could cold call, walking in on people, that he would make a good mortgage banker. Keith hired him as an analyst, and Kyle grew within the company from that point on.

An analyst is one of three basic mortgage banking positions. An analyst evaluates and packages new loan opportunities. A "producer" is the term for the people who originate loans. That was Keith's job in the company, and that of other individuals within the office. The "closer" handles the paperwork to complete the deal and the servicing component. Patti did that job. That servicing component is important because it defines the difference between a mortgage broker and a mortgage banker, like Kyle.

The nature of the mortgage banking industry almost makes teamwork mandatory. Kyle explains the necessity of teamwork this way:

> In the commercial real estate finance business, most of the lenders are out of state, and firms represent them, not individual producers. Lending programs, underwriting guidelines, and market assumptions are constantly changing. Even the most talented producer could not retain all of the specifics, so sharing is vital for success. Keith was an individual producer. He originated his own loans and earned his own fees, but we always worked as a team.
>
> The lending market is too large and complex for any one person to master. Though there are categories of loan types, the number and variety of capital sources in the marketplace requires constant diligence and cooperation among the entire team. Anytime we had a deal come in, Keith would call me into his office and say, 'I've got a loan opportunity. Here it is. What do you think?'
>
> After discussing the transaction, Keith would say, "Kyle, can you package it? Can you review the operating statements? Can you create the loan submission?" Once the loan submission was created, Keith would review and identify my grammar or underwriting mistakes. He had a red pen and graded my work

as if I were in grade school. I hated that red pen my first year in business, but he taught me commercial real estate finance one deal at a time. That's how I learned the business. Keith was an amazing mentor and teacher. I owe my career to his excellent tutelage. I have a red pen in my desk, ready to use on the next loan package an analyst brings me.

Kyle may have started working as an analyst, but soon he was pushing Keith to let him go out and source business on his own. Keith added "production assistant" to Kyle's duties, and Kyle kept doing analyst work for Keith. Within a year, Kyle was on his own as a producer. Two years later he was on full commission.

Kyle was showing lots of that "pluck," the hard work that Horatio Alger wrote about, but now there was a little luck, too. General Motors Acceptance Corporation (GMAC), the largest mortgage banking firm in the U.S. at the time, was going to acquire the firm where Keith and Kyle worked.

Fortunately, Keith had the foresight to know that GMAC would never give someone Kyle's age a full-time producer role and the title that might go with it. So right before the acquisition took place, Keith gave Kyle an assistant VP title. They hired another person as an analyst to support the two of them. Kyle was successful at GMAC and had become a full vice president before he left.

THE EVOLUTION BEGINS—TIME TO HIRE

Kyle and Keith left GMAC in 2006 to form Commercial Capital Advisors, known as CommCap Advisors. Keith and Kyle were now equal partners with Patti as the closer.

Kyle was and remains very active in NAIOP, The Commercial Real Estate Development Association, where he's served in several leadership roles. He noticed a young man that came to all the meetings and was often the last person to leave. Kyle thought it was great that a college student would make the effort to come to meetings and volunteer. This young man's name was Matthew Hoyt. Kyle describes what he liked about Matthew:

He was a college kid and probably owned one dress shirt and one pair of dress slacks. He was coming to professional meetings without knowing anyone. He just showed up to meet people and volunteer.

I take pride in trying to hire people from UNLV. I want to support the University and community. Matthew fit the bill. His father was a Real Estate Finance professor. He was involved with NAIOP. He was involved with the Lied Institute for Real Estate Studies. More importantly, he was willing to be in uncomfortable situations, which would be necessary if he moved beyond the analyst role. I liked his hunger.

You must be able to handle uncomfortable situations in sales. Sensing the awkwardness and using it as an opportunity to forge a new relationship or separate yourself from competitors is vital. Often, you are most successful when other people are uncomfortable. It's sad but true.

Kyle has found that a willingness to persevere and the ability to be comfortable in uncomfortable situations are traits that make for success in his business. Over the years, he's had several unsuccessful hires. When he described a few of them to me, I immediately understood what he saw in Matthew.

He's hired people who were successful bank loan officers, but who didn't work out at CommCap. They sat and waited for the phone to ring, instead of hitting the street and the phone to generate business. And they weren't willing to do that hard work of learning about all the packages of the capital sources used by CommCap.

Another person who didn't work out was really smart and well educated, with a Master's in Economics. But he didn't have any drive, any compelling reason to succeed. He was comfortable being where he was. Kyle prefers to build his team with people who are looking to personally grow.

This is not a problem unique to Kyle. A number of our mortgage banker/broker/capital service clients have had similar experiences. This is another reason it is essential to properly screen, filter, and establish expectations prior to adding to your team.

Matthew had the right stuff. He had lots of drive and perseverance.

In 2007, Keith and Kyle hired him to be their analyst. He would review the raw data, operating statements and rent rolls and prepare the loan submission package. Keith and Kyle would usually discuss it, talk about the deal, and then submit it to their lenders for review.

Matthew is still with the firm today, but it hasn't been easy. Right after he was hired, the market went south.

LEADING IN A DOWN MARKET

The downturn was tough on everyone. There was a year and half where Keith and Kyle didn't pay themselves anything. There were days when the phone didn't ring once.

Kyle had been in the business for a decade by then. He was active in NAIOP and the community. He had existing clients. He was calling, but no one was calling him back. There just wasn't any business.

It was even tougher on Matthew, who didn't have Kyle's experience or clients. And because there were no deals for him to learn from, his training cycle was extended by several years.

In 2010, the heart of the downturn, Kyle hired Adam Gregory. On the face of it, that makes little sense. Take it as the first example of how Kyle does things that aren't "normal." Here's how it happened.

Keith and Kyle were sharing office space with another commercial mortgage company. That firm focused on smaller-balance multi-family loans, while CommCap concentrated on industrial, retail, office and multifamily loans in excess of $5 million. The idea was that the two firms could share referrals and perhaps even merge. That never happened.

The benefits they hoped for didn't materialize, and the firms discovered that their business practices and styles were very different. The other firm worked mostly with smaller apartment owners, while CommCap worked with large institutional borrowers. The other firm was more like a broker; they would obtain a loan request from a borrower, then ship it out to as many people as they could. CommCap is a mortgage banker. They have lenders, like life insurance companies, that they represent exclusively.

Even though they liked the people in the other firm and got along well, eventually Keith and Kyle decided to take separate office space.

Shortly after that, Adam, who was with the other firm, called Kyle and said he'd like to switch firms. Adam realized that if he didn't represent lenders in the marketplace, and lenders were hard to find because there was a credit crunch, he needed to be somewhere there were lenders.

Kyle thought Adam would be a good fit. While the two firms shared space, Adam spent a lot of time talking with Kyle, wanting to work on larger deals and split fees. He was coming up as an analyst and also originating and closing his own loans. So Kyle knew about his abilities and work ethic.

There was another plus that Kyle saw in Adam: "You could tell immediately that Adam came from wealth." For Kyle, who grew up south of Gary, that was a plus because "when people with money walked in the room, they would instantly connect with Adam. He was already in the club, the club that I was not a part of." So there were some big plusses, but there were also issues.

Kyle was friends with the owners of the other company and he didn't want to do anything that would damage that relationship. In the end he called the owners and told them that Adam wanted to come over and that he wanted Adam, but that he wouldn't hire Adam without their permission. They weren't thrilled about it, but they gave Kyle and Adam their blessing and Adam joined CommCap in 2010 as a producer. This is just one example of how Kyle is a consummate professional.

BECOMING HIS OWN BOSS

In 2012 the market started to pick up, and Keith and Kyle discovered that they had very different ideas about what to do next. Keith was coming to the end of his career and thinking about retirement. Kyle figured that they were at the bottom of a downturn in the economy and it was the perfect time to grow. They both wound up getting what they wanted.

Keith and Patti retired and moved back East. He started out as semi-retired and did a few deals before he retired for good at the end of 2014. Kyle bought Keith's half of the business and immediately had to face two challenges.

He had to find someone to do the closer/office manager work. Patti connected him with the daughter of a friend who was a CPA and at a difficult time in her life and career. Kyle hired her. But that still left him with the need to replace Keith as a producer.

Kyle figured that Matthew was already working as a part-time producer and was ready to move into a production role full time. But that meant he had to hire a new analyst so Matthew could concentrate on originating deals. He tried the traditional channels without much luck. He started asking friends and colleagues for ideas. One of them suggested Shelly Dunbar.

Kyle had met Shelly several years before; Kyle was serving as Chairman of the Executive Council for the UNLV Lied Institute of Real Estate Studies when Shelly was a student there. It turned out that she was ready for something new. Kyle made her an offer, and she joined the team as the analyst. After one year at CommCap, she is working hard and pushing for a production role.

By the end of 2014, the CPA found a position with a higher salary that was also a better fit for her education and skills. Kyle was left with another tough decision. He had to find someone to handle the office management, but he really wanted more than an admin. The company was slowly growing, and he was spending more time working with the other producers and training Shelly than in sourcing new loans.

CommCap maintains extensive data on the history of their loan production. Kyle calls it his "real analytics of mortgage banking." When he analyzed the data, he saw that the company's most successful years were when Matthew was supporting the production team and when Kyle was spending more time originating business. This is yet another example of Kyle's excellent team leadership. He allocated the time to analyze when and how the team was producing at its highest level and identified who was filling which roles.

Kyle knew that Matthew was trustworthy, reliable and detailed oriented, but moving him to a new role would be big change. After much deliberation, Kyle offered Matthew the new position of Director of Operations. Matthew would be responsible for running the company, overseeing the servicing portfolio, closing new loans, marketing and training, but still have the flexibility to work with his existing clients. They agreed to a pay package that matched the management and production components of the position. As of 2015, Matthew is excelling at the position, Kyle is free to hunt for more deals, and CommCap loan production is up.

———————•———————

If you are looking for assistance in the recruiting, selection and hiring process, please visit
www.massimo-group.com/consulting

———————•———————

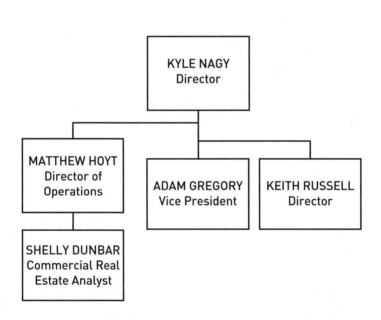

Commercial Capital Advisors organizational chart

DOING THINGS DIFFERENTLY

Many people associate the sentiment "Normal sucks!" with Dave Ramsey, who popularized it promoting his programs for helping people get control of their finances. But that's a motto that Kyle was living by, way before he took Dave Ramsey's course. Here's Kyle's thinking:

> All relationships are either declining or improving. They require constant work and attention. Your relationships should grow stronger over time and become more meaningful and fulfilling. Businesses are the same way. You can either invest in constant improvement or accept the normal and status quo. If you believe your company is just fine today the way it is, you are already in decline and do not know it yet. I am not suggesting you have to be consistently growing the size or scope of the company, but you can constantly improve your services or processes. If you do not, someone who is hungrier and willing to work harder is coming for your clients. We try to think what other people are doing and then do something different.

That means "something different" in every area of the business. CommCap's compensation isn't "normal," but it reflects Kyle's values and what he wants from the team.

Nevada law mandates that everyone who works at CommCap must be a W2 employee, and that's different from most firms outside the state. CommCap gives people 401(K) matching, but where things move beyond normal is when it comes to bonuses.

Kyle wants the people who work at CommCap to be improving themselves. So they can earn a bigger bonus if they take a self-improvement class or work on a graduate degree during the previous quarter. That's not normal. Kyle wants them to be part of the community, so they can pick up an extra bonus if they do a charitable event in the previous quarter. That's not normal, either.

Neither is the way that CommCap handles team events. For most of the other teams in this book, "team events" fall into two groups. Some events are "team building" events, formal sessions designed to increase teamwork and productivity. Other events are "family" events, usually dinners where spouses or whole families join the team. That's how CommCap used to do their team events. Here's how Kyle describes what they decided to do instead:

> We decided to ditch the spouses for a day of debauchery and fun, going to an extended lunch, playing golf, going to a UNLV basketball game, doing something different outside of the office without work and without the spouses. The goal is to build relationship with fellow team members beyond the office environment and without a corporate structure. We do not have to spend our weekends together, but we should invest in each other's lives.

Like other teams we've looked at in this book, CommCap has a regular production meeting. They hold their meeting every 2 weeks. If one of their lenders is coming to town, the team has another meeting to plan for the event.

The normal practice for most mortgage bankers is that the person who is assigned to the lender handles the visit. But at CommCap they do something that's not normal. At CommCap, everyone goes to meet the lender. That's more expensive, but Kyle thinks it's worth it.

The planning meeting is to make sure everyone is up to speed on everything relevant about the lender and the relationship. Kyle wants to be certain that:

> Everyone understands the personality of this lender and has updated information about why is he coming out and what his family is up to. The goal is to have a more personal conversation with him, rather than just talking about deals.
>
> We also try to incorporate an activity that plays to the personality of our guest. If it is their first visit to the market, we have a gift basket delivered to their hotel room with Vegas chocolates, souvenirs, dice, or playing cards.

CommCap is always looking for a way to do things that will give them an edge in their basic business cycle. Kyle thinks the way they work together physically is one of those things:

> The work environment is open compared to other mortgage bankers. Though each producer has their own office, the doors remain open at all time and we comment on each other's conversations. We executed a new lease with very favorable terms at the bottom of the market. If office space was expensive, we'd all be in the bullpen and be fine with it.
>
> We want to hear what people are talking about. When Adam is on the phone talking with one of our lenders I need to speak with, I'll just walk into his office and sit down. I'll hear some of his conversation. Adam will put us on speakerphone and we'll talk to the lender together.
>
> Lending relationships are shared relationships. The strength of the relationship is based upon how many times we can touch that lender. We are constantly talking about lenders and the programs. Our success as mortgage bankers depends upon understanding the lending environment and characteristics of our lenders.

WINNING THE BUSINESS

Kyle describes what CommCap does as "originate, underwrite, close and service commercial loans." It's a team effort, where individuals represent the firm. Here's how the process works.

Through associations like CCIM, SIOR, and NAIOP, as well as UNLV, CommCap has a presence in all areas of the commercial real estate community. Opportunities come from their connections and presence.

Once they have an opportunity, they start to package it. That usually involves a lot of discussion and brainstorming. They contact potential lenders, such as life insurance companies, and provide the loan submission package to solicit quotes.

When they have obtained a favorable quote, they will present it to the borrower. If the borrower likes it, too, then it's time for an application, deposits, and the start of the closing process. When the loan closes, CommCap gets a fee and the originator takes his or her split.

If the lender is a life insurance company, CommCap retains the servicing rights, which means they either collect the mortgage payment, taxes and insurance, or they do an annual financial and physical inspection. In either scenario, the lender is paying CommCap an annual servicing fee.

FACILITATION THROUGH TEAMWORK

As we touched upon earlier in this chapter, professional mortgage banking almost mandates a team effort. I asked Kyle to give me some more detail on how the team works together to meet the borrower's needs and close the deal.

Kyle said that, when any producer brings a deal, that deal is their deal for compensation purposes, even though putting it all together is a team effort. When they meet with a brokerage firm or large developer, they do it as a team:

> I bring the entire production staff. We all speak at different parts of the meeting. We each present a property type or lending program. Everyone gets an opportunity to speak and try to build a relationship with the individuals in the room.

When a producer brings a deal to the team, the producer manages the client relationship, asking for help if needed. But the team manages the lenders collectively, which leads to a lot of discussion about lenders and their programs. Sometimes that happens in a production meeting, but often the conversations are informal.

The conversations and back and forth help CommCap come up with the best possible solution for the borrower, but the conversations have another benefit. They also help the team and the team members improve their game.

When I interviewed Kyle, Shelly was learning how to be a good analyst. The deals the team works are the way she learns. Other team members turn some of their conversations into coaching and training sessions. And every team member learns from the discussions that go on with every deal.

Kyle and CommCap are constantly searching for ways to get better and get an edge on the competition. Sometimes the search for a better way starts with an uncomfortable moment.

IDENTIFYING DIFFERENTIATORS

One of the firm's current projects is developing a CRM system to give CommCap an edge on the competition throughout the business cycle. The project started when Kyle and Keith noticed a problem.

Every year at the Mortgage Bankers Association conference, they would meet with their lenders to review performance. They were aggressively seeking opportunities and presenting them to lenders, but the review meetings were often uncomfortable; a lender might ask why they didn't do any deals in the prior year, and the best Kyle could say was that they'd contacted the lender and nothing hit. Kyle realized that they needed some kind of tracking system.

Matthew cobbled together the first version using Excel. Now they could track every opportunity, including the source of the lead, the borrower's preferred lending source, the type of property and the location. The lender conferences were a whole new experience.

Now when the lenders asked a question, Kyle had numbers. He could push back by demonstrating how much business CommCap was doing and what kind and where. But there was still something missing.

The next round of improvement was to develop the ability to tie properties, borrowers and lenders together. Kyle likes to say that "mortgage banking is a relationship business," and his new CRM system was helping him manage those relationships with borrowers and with lenders. It's helping him master the details so he can make those relationships productive.

The system gives CommCap a competitive advantage in several ways. Marketing is much more efficient because it can be more targeted. Analysis benefits from quick access to details of prior deals. And, of course, lender conferences are more productive.

The CRM system is still a work in progress. Kyle estimates that they were 50% there.

Kyle says that mortgage banking is behind other commercial real estate professions when it comes to using technology, so there really aren't models for him to copy. But he believes that that the CRM system will completely change the way CommCap does business and give them a huge competitive advantage.

Unfortunately, technology is always growing and always improving, so Kyle knows he will never reach 100%—nor will anyone else. But unlike the average commercial real estate professional, Kyle is always striving for improvement.

———————◆———————

If you too are striving for improvement, perhaps it's time to invest in your greatest asset—you. We also coach mortgage brokers and bankers. To learn more, visit **www.massimo-group.com**

———————◆———————

BUILDING ON RELATIONSHIPS

Kyle says that "mortgage banking is a relationship business," but you don't have to hear him say it to know he believes it. You can tell by watching how he acts. Relationships with lenders are important, but so are the relationships that tie CommCap to the community and the relationships with friends and colleagues. The effectiveness of the team is tied to the way the members work together, so relationships and fit are important.

Kyle hires people on gut feel. That means some don't work out; but once he finds someone with drive and perseverance, he works hard to help them succeed. In fact, during our interview he said, "I look at CommCap as a vehicle for all of us to find success." Once more, you don't have to listen to what he says to know he believes that. You can observe how he acts.

On many teams, it's expected that people will be responsible for their own development. They take courses if they choose and join associations. But on this team, personal development is baked into the work and expectations.

The bonus system rewards behaviors that build relationships and help develop skills. Daily work is structured around team success, and roles can change as people develop or if business needs change. Kyle and Keith took extra time to help Matthew learn the business, even though the downturn made that harder. Later, as business needs changed, Matthew's role changed as well.

Nothing sums up what's special about this team more than the mantra, "Normal sucks!" The team's work environment is different from that of most teams in their industry. There's a bonus for self-development and for community service. When a lender comes to town, he or she meets with the whole team, not just one producer. They're putting time and resources into developing a CRM system that will give them a powerful competitive advantage.

"Normal sucks!" drives an incessant quest to improve and do things differently.

IN HIS OWN WORDS

Kyle Nagy

> I would say that you pick your team based upon people who are driven to be successful, not driven to be wealthy or make a name for themselves. People who work for the sole purpose of being successful and finding joy in it are the kind of people we want at CommCap.
>
> I have had potential employees end an interview with, 'I cannot wait to start working for you and make a lot of money.' I know at that moment, they are not the right person for CommCap. If you love what you do and find joy in it, success and wealth will be the byproduct. Diligently work each day to improve, and you will never be concerned with money again.

Kyle Nagy certainly does several things differently from other teams in this book, but it's not simply about doing his own thing.

He's convinced that you gain competitive advantage if you're different in the right ways. He thinks through the things he does, and he only does things that are true to his values. And, this may be the biggest lesson: He changes what he's doing if it's not working.

NEXT UP

Cathy Jones is the team leader featured in our next profile, and she has a dual challenge. She's the owner of a commercial real estate firm and she's also the team leader of one of the firm's internal teams. This is an intricate balance to which any owner/producer can relate. We will introduce the "Three Ring Circus" and how you can be the ringmaster!

INVESTMENT SERVICES GROUP

The Role of a Team Leader

Team Size: 4
Market: Las Vegas, Nevada
Focus: Commercial Real Estate Sales and Leasing

Most of the profiles in this book are about teams, some that were started by two or more peers who said something like, "Hey, we like and respect each other and we've got a good mix of skills. Let's get together and combine our efforts." Sometimes, that led to the formalization of responsibilities, and in some cases to the creation of a separate entity altogether. It was a bit different for Cathy Jones and Paul Miachika.

In their case, their broker/manager brought them together, with the idea that they could be a great team. At the time, no one knew that was the first step in the creation of a dominant, independent, team in Las Vegas commercial real estate.

Cathy Jones is a CPA who originally worked in the title insurance business. In 2003, seeking to expand her abilities, develop more personal relationships, and leverage the ties she had already developed, she joined a commercial brokerage firm with common ownership in Las Vegas and Phoenix, Arizona.

At the time, her broker was focused on building teams because he thought an effective team could outperform the individual production of the team members. He wanted to form a commercial investment team, and after consulting with the other owners he identified another experienced agent in the Phoenix office who would be a good fit for this new team. At that point, Cathy, Paul Miachika and a third agent in Las Vegas came together to work as a team. The broker thought the three shared a similar vision, yet had different sets of qualities and attributes and skills. He sat them down and outlined a plan to form a commercial investment brokerage team.

Paul was located in Phoenix, Arizona, while Cathy and the other associate were in Las Vegas, Nevada. With their broker's help, they mapped out how they thought they could make the whole thing work. As Paul reflects:

> It probably took us about a month to figure out how we were going to work together. We developed a sort of flow chart of how we were going to win business, how we were going to put deals together, how we were going to get them closed. We went through each of those steps, breaking down the details of what we really had to do and who was best at doing what.

Paul is very good at analysis and a master of the details of fulfilling business. He wasn't as natural, however, at finding and winning business as were his other two team members. In a team, that challenge could become irrelevant if team members possess complementary strengths. In this case, the other brokers could concentrate on things they liked to do and did well, and Paul could do more of the things he did well. And the team would benefit because everything would be done better.

In the beginning, they planned for Cathy to handle contract conversion while Paul would handle the number crunching and keeping projects on track. The other broker would be the finder who would go out and get the business. That changed fairly quickly.

It turned out that Cathy was very good at finding business. She was naturally assertive and fairly social, two common traits you will tend to see in top performers. The strong network she had developed in her previous work helped a lot as well. The team was further defined when the third broker, who was also the manager of the Las Vegas office, determined he needed to spend more time fulfilling that role. The commercial real estate investment team of this residential firm was now Cathy and Paul. Within 2 years, they were a top performing team in the company.

DECISION TIME

At this point, there was a change in the senior management structure of their firm. It's natural for top producing professionals to evaluate their situation and think about other possibilities. Cathy and Paul had two concerns: First, they felt they were providing their company far more in revenue than the resources and referrals the company was providing for them. Second, they felt the office did not provide the working environment they were looking for in a firm.

They discussed these concerns with their existing firm, and after evaluating the responses, the decision was made to move on. Cathy had become the team leader and felt she could enhance her commercial investment brokerage opportunities by starting her own firm. She recognized that her commercial practice had been very successful and was confident she could create a successful new brand and name for herself and her team.

Cathy and Paul formed Sun Commercial Real Estate, Inc. in 2006, which, at the time of formation, consisted of Cathy and Paul's investment team and one other land agent. Since then it has turned into a full-service brokerage firm that Cathy owns 100%. In addition to being Cathy's partner in their investment team that they call the Investment Services Group (ISG), Paul is also the designated broker of the Arizona office. Cathy is the president of the firm, the designated broker in Nevada and the team leader of the ISG. As all owner/producers can attest, this is a challenging position. There is a never-ending battle to balance the roles of operator and generator. Cathy found a way to balance both and build not only a dominant team but also a significant brokerage firm.

THE TEAM LEADER'S ROLE—A THREE RING CIRCUS

Cathy, like all owners of companies who also have production responsibilities, has a professional life defined by the "Three Ring Circus."

As owner and president of Sun Commercial, she is responsible for operating, generating and facilitating business in the company. This includes:

- Financial oversight
- Sales oversight
- Marketing programs
- Human resource
- Systems integration

As the team leader of the Investment Services Group, she's responsible for overall team performance and also for finding, winning and overseeing fulfillment of business for the team. This includes

- Prospecting programs
- Sales presentations
- Personal and team branding
- Personal and team networking
- Process integration

As the manager of both the firm and the team, Cathy is responsible for recruiting strategy and support, training programs, sales/team meetings, sales management and policy implementation. This includes all facets of

- Recruiting
- Hiring
- Training
- Motivating
- Retaining

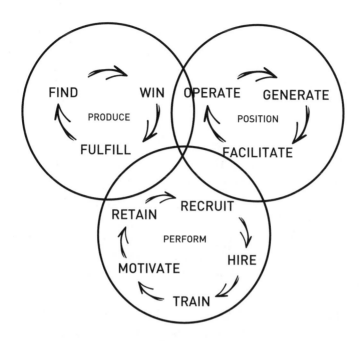

The Team Leader's Role - The Three Ring Circus

Juggling these three roles is quite a challenge. In the beginning, Cathy worked at building the company around the success of the ISG. For the first few years of Sun Commercial, the Las Vegas and Phoenix markets were active and the company got off to a strong start. Cathy was able to balance her role of company president and team leader. Then came the Fall of 2008 and the start of the Great Recession.

THRIVING IN A MARKET DOWNTURN

In a business downturn, companies have to adapt to changing conditions quickly. Firms that don't recognize what's happening or that don't adapt quickly, simply disappear. The first decision most team leaders and company owners make at this time to is how to simply stay alive. Team leaders have to find or even create opportunities and determine not only how to survive but how to thrive in a major downturn. There are several strategies team leaders should implement in order to thrive during these low-velocity market cycles.

Teams that thrive in significant downturns prepare for the inevitable end of a growing market. There is a reason squirrels collect nuts in the fall and bears consume most of their calories before winter. They know what's ahead.

Only a handful of brokers predicted the depth and duration of the Great Recession, and far fewer prepared for it. It is the responsibility of business owners and team leaders to strategize for the reduction in market activity. That's why they are "leaders" and not simply producers. There should be a proactive plan, budgeted savings, and prepared marketing initiatives to quickly address these opportunities as the market shifts.

It is a sad but true fact that most companies, teams and team members make their greatest mistakes when things are good, and they do not plan for a significant drop in their usual transaction volume.

Teams that thrive in significant downturns adapt their strategy to the conditions. You have to find business in unfamiliar places and pursue it aggressively. For Sun Commercial, the strategy became trying to get business from the REO departments of larger lenders. This actually meant spending more time and money on marketing and business development efforts.

This is a contrarian view but one that is applied by the most successful firms. When everyone else is simply trying to survive and cutting every cost they can think of, more successful firms identify opportunities and pursue them vigorously.

For Cathy and Sun Commercial, this meant calling and calling and calling on lenders that might provide some business. It meant climbing into the car and driving to California to perform listing presentations. It meant doing lots of monotonous Broker Price Opinion work. It meant marketing to owners and pursuing leasing opportunities to generate at least some income.

Teams that thrive in significant downturns pay ferocious attention to business basics. When times are good, it's human nature to get a little fat, to spend a little more than you have to or take on projects that are marginal. When a downturn hits, the margin of error evaporates and you have to pay attention to how you approach every day.

Cathy says they were able to keep the doors open and the lights on by reinforcing fundamentals and operating proactively, knowing their income would drop significantly. That was hard on her and Paul, but it was even harder on the junior brokers who had joined the company.

As the Great Recession continued, Cathy's strategy paid off. The firm has solidified its position in the market as a resource for property owners in good times and in bad. Unfortunately, but not surprisingly, some team members, like tens of thousands across the country, were not in a position to survive the downturn in business. Sun Commercial was now the same firm as when they were starting out prior to the Great Recession and the focus was on Cathy's team—the Investment Services Group.

Just getting through the downturn isn't enough. You have to pay attention to the things that will position you for great success when times get better. You have to work to make sure you maintain relationships with the clients you want to do business with and hang onto as many good people as you can.

It turned out that there was one benefit that came out of the recession. Cathy and her team performed many Broker Price Opinions and did a lot of number crunching, and they got very good at it. Their clients began to see that as a strength of the team, one that will be a competitive advantage as business continues to come back.

Cathy did something that successful businesses do in a downturn. The consulting firm of Bain & Company studied performance during a downturn. They discovered that recessions are hard on everyone, but they're much harder on firms that don't adjust. And some firms, like Cathy's, actually develop strengths in a downturn that boost their performance when times get better.

When the market starts to recover, you have readjust your strategy. You have to add people and other resources for increased business. As of today, Sun Commercial Real Estate, Inc. has fifteen brokers and two support staff.

HIRING AND RETAINING GOOD PEOPLE

Hiring is one of the hardest things to get right. At a glance, it looks easy: Just go out and hire great people. But it's not easy at all, as Cathy discovered early.

She had formed Sun Commercial, and the firm was having a lot of initial success. This success attracted the attention of brokers in the area:

> We started having people call me and ask if I would consider letting them join the firm. Honestly, I think initially I wasn't careful about that. What I mean by that is, I didn't really think through a plan, if you will, on who came in.
>
> So there were some agents that came in and went because they didn't fit the value system that I have and the culture of our company.

The result was a lot of turnover. That's not good for the team or the people who are coming and then going. Cathy's experience illustrates something that can make hiring the right people hard and very frustrating.

You must consider two things when you hire a new person for your team. Most team leaders get one of them right away. They understand that you want top performers, people who have the history or demonstrated potential to do great work.

Fit is the other dimension, and it's critical. If your new team member doesn't have the skills and personality to fit into the team and make the team more productive, you've got a bad hire. Cathy has learned from her experience and hires differently now. Here's an example.

Cathy met Roy Fritz in the course of business. At the time, he was working for another firm, and he had the opportunity to list a small industrial building. That wasn't the kind of business he was doing, so he contacted Cathy and asked if Sun Commercial could list it and pay him a referral.

When the property sold, she took Roy to lunch as a thank you for the listing, but also to evaluate him as a possible addition to her team. He had good prospecting skills and a lot of connections and experience. Cathy thought he could help build the non-REO business that was beginning to come back.

When she broached the subject of joining the team, Roy said he was interested. Once, that might have been enough. Once, Cathy might have made the hiring decision on her own. But now the whole team is involved in the hiring process.

Many larger companies known for their excellent HR practices make interviews with members of the work team part of their process. At Southwest Airlines, every candidate is interviewed by groups of people who will work with a person, as well as by people who already do the job the candidate is seeking. At Whole Foods, the hiring decision is made by the team the candidate will join if he or she is hired.

Using team interviews gives those companies and Sun Commercial two important advantages. The first is multiple perceptions of the candidate.

When only one person does the interviewing, it's easy to miss things. Candidates are on their best behavior, and first impressions count for more than they should. With team interviewing, only one person at a time may be asking the questions, but everyone in the interview is observing the candidate.

Team interviews also give candidates the opportunity to ask questions about the team and the company. That allows for an important discussion of team values and culture. Team members have the opportunity to share their perspectives of why the company is a great place to work for, as well as what kind of people and behaviors fit best.

When a new person is hired, he or she signs a contract that specifies how everyone is compensated. Having this kind of "open book" helps prevent misunderstandings and suspicion.

A new broker just starting in the business gets a base salary and a very small percentage of every transaction that the team closes. They've given new brokers just starting out the option of a higher percentage and no base, but so far no one has taken them up on the offer.

When the team closes a deal, everyone gets a fixed percentage of it. If it's a sale, the splits are one way. On a lease transaction, the junior agents on the team make more. There's also an origination bonus when a team member procures a new business opportunity. Cathy does not participate in the origination bonus, but she does have the highest split.

Cathy wants the people who work at Sun Commercial to continue their education. She's constantly encouraging them to work toward their CCIM or take a class that will help them do their work better. She also sees coaching team members as part of her role:

> When I see somebody not handling something the way I think would be best, I try to make sure I immediately take the time to talk through how they could have done it a little bit differently and why I think that would be a good way to approach it.

Cathy also retains the services of a coaching organization to assist her with the management of her team, as well as to work with the individual team members. This approach has allowed all members of the team to define the vision of the team, define the roles of the individual team members to achieve this vision and create specific metrics to ensure all team members fulfill their respective roles.

———•———

Most, but not all the teams in this book retain a coaching relationship in one form or another. A couple of the teams profiled herein retain the Massimo Group for their coaching needs. The ISG team is one such team. For more information on our coaching services, please visit **www.massimo-group.com/coaching**

———•———

Cathy also sets the example when it comes to networking and building relationships. She's active in CCIM, where she's served on the board and been president of the local chapter. She's also active in the United Way and networking groups.

The goal is to create a team full of hard-working people with common values and complementary skills and experience. That's what you want when it's time to do business. Here's what the ISG Team looks like today.

THE ISG TEAM

The Investment Service Group team at Sun Commercial has five core members. Here's a summary of how Cathy defines each role.

Cathy A. Jones: Team Leader, Marketing and Conversion Specialist
This position's primary focus is to develop and convert new business relationships, as well as provide team leadership.

Paul Miachika: Senior Broker, Conversion & Service Delivery Specialist
This position's focus is to manage the financial analysis of all investment properties for both listings and buyer acquisition opportunities and to handle contractual documentation. Paul also manages transactions from listing to closing.

Roy Fritz: Senior Associate, Marketing & Conversion Specialist
This position's focus is to assist in both marketing and conversion phases of team transactions.

Jessica Cegavske: Senior Associate, Conversion, Service Delivery & Financial Analyst
This position's focus is to assist in the conversion and service delivery phase of team transactions through closing.

Junior Leasing Agent & Research Specialist
This position's focus is to take the lead on Junior Leasing assignments and research potential investment-listing and buyer-acquisition opportunities.

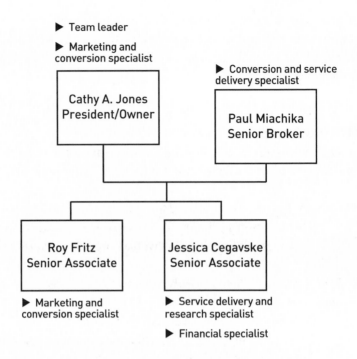

▶ Team leader

▶ Marketing and conversion specialist

▶ Conversion and service delivery specialist

Cathy A. Jones
President/Owner

Paul Miachika
Senior Broker

Roy Fritz
Senior Associate

Jessica Cegavske
Senior Associate

▶ Marketing and conversion specialist

▶ Service delivery and research specialist

▶ Financial specialist

Investment Services Group organizational chart

MANAGING AN OPPORTUNITY

The team leader must set the expectations for processing every opportunity the team will secure. Every team does things slightly differently.

Some teams have defined roles where people do the same thing on every transaction, while others define a "point person" for each transaction. The point person is the team member responsible for successfully managing the opportunity, with help from the team, from start to finish. The point person may or may not be the single point of contact for the client as well. Some teams, like the ISG team, take a hybrid approach.

Everything starts with financial analysis. For a typical investment sale, they do a complete workup, including discounted cash flow analysis, a sales comparison analysis and a comparison of different methods for valuing a property. They consider which approach carries the most weight with the types of buyers they think will be interested in that property. It's a group process. Here's how Cathy describes their process to me:

> When we are doing our Argus analysis, for example, we will sit down as a team. We are looking at the lease comps, the sale comps. We look at the particular sub market, location of the asset, those sorts of things, and we ask ourselves if we're comfortable that we are going to use $1.25 for lease rates for these four spaces that are vacant and how long we think it's going to take to lease out.

Obviously they won't always agree at first. So they talk it through until they come to an agreement. Then the person doing the analysis (Paul or Jessica) moves on with the Argus run and with what the team has decided.

If it's a larger investment sale, then one of team members, usually Cathy, takes the lead on the listing. But there's still a lot of team participation:

> We sit down as a team and create a strategy on how we are going to market the property. And then typically everybody—myself, Roy, Paul and Jess—identifies buyers we would want to market that property to, as an early look.

The company has a marketing person who puts the package together. Some of the information will be provided by company staff. The ISG provides the Argus runs, the rent rolls and sale and lease comps. They outline the details of the investment. Then the marketing person puts everything together.

Cathy says that she's "picky" about the marketing packages. She usually gets involved in editing the final draft along with Paul or Jess or Roy, depending on who takes the lead on the package. Once the package passes her scrutiny, it's ready to be sent to the identified buyer pool.

If the property doesn't sell to someone in the initial buyer pool, the firm promotes it to their larger database of investors and then, if necessary, through other listing services. The decision on where to go next and when is a team decision.

Cathy usually stays involved until a deal's business points are agreed to and then hands the project off to Paul. He makes sure the purchase agreement is negotiated and executed. He makes sure the earnest money deposit is received and all the due diligence materials are delivered to the buyer. He also deals with any questions the buyer may have along the way.

Typically, once they've closed on a transaction, Jessica provides all the necessary information to the company marketing team and helps them draft a promotion piece to publicize the sale. There's one more thing:

> Then, of course, we celebrate. Admittedly, we need to do a better job in this area, but we do take the time to acknowledge the good work the team has completed for our client and for ourselves.

This is one area in which many teams, and especially team leaders, fail. Like Cathy Jones, team leaders must be the biggest cheerleaders, the vanguards of momentum, motivation and celebration.

IN THEIR OWN WORDS

Cathy Jones

> When you are bringing someone new into the mix, you are typically doing that with a preconceived idea of what that person's strengths are going to be and where they are going to fit into the team. But sometimes that person doesn't always fit in exactly where you thought they would. You have to have some flexibility on moving responsibilities around to be able to respond to the different skill sets.
>
> My first hire is a good example. He was a door-to-door suit salesman who sold a suit to a broker in our office. And the broker

said "You really should talk to that kid; he's a great salesman."

So I really liked him and I hired him, thinking that he would help on the sales side in generating new business and making cold calls and all that. But I quickly figured out that he was really a behind-the-scenes guy. He was with me for 8 great years, and he probably would have been here longer if it wasn't for the Great Recession.

Paul Miachika

When I asked Paul for his one piece of advice, he offered the following based on the book, The Boys in the Boat by Daniel James Brown, about the University of Washington's eight-man rowing team that won Olympic gold at Berlin in 1936:

> Everyone on that team is different, but at the same time they have all got to pull together as one. If they don't do that, they are not very successful. I think that's probably a great metaphor for any great team. All these individuals have a special job. From the outside, it looks seamless if they're doing it right. But really it's made of a bunch of all these individuals working together.
>
> Ultimately, you've got to let yourself go and just be part of the team. Everyone else depends on you; you can't let anybody else down. These rowers call that "getting the swing." All of a sudden they are just all working like clockwork together. And when you do that you never lose a race. That's the way a great team should be.

The Investment Services Group is a team where everyone uses their unique skills to help the team succeed. It's one of only two teams in this book with a virtual team member, Paul. Even though his number-crunching work is ideally suited to working at a distance, he still makes regular trips to Las Vegas for face time with other team members.

NEXT UP

The next team is one of the largest teams in the book, in the largest market in North America. It's a great example of how a team can evolve over time. Their story is a good example of how a few key decisions can make a big difference, and of how a top producer can struggle at first but then evolve to make the transition to team leader.

TEAM NELSON

Time for the Client

Team Size: 8
Market: New York, New York
Focus: Investment Sales Brokerage

The best team leaders in the business are ruthlessly effective managers of their own time and that of their team. The catch is that managing your time effectively as an individual producer is different from managing your time as a team leader. Learning the difference is the journey that James Nelson has been on for the last several years. How the team spends their time is focused on one objective, servicing their clients.

James joined Massey Knakal (which at the time of this book's publication was recently purchased by Cushman & Wakefield) right out of college. He transitioned to full-time sales in 2000 and was involved in more than $100 million worth of business in the next 2 years. That performance earned him the New York Real Estate Board's (REBNY) "Most Promising Rookie Salesperson of the Year" Award. That was just the start. The rewards and recognition for James and his team have continued to pile up.

James became the youngest partner in Massey Knakal history in 2004. That's when he took on a part-time associate. The associate did things to support James's individual work, like showing properties, underwriting and helping with evaluations and marketing books. That made a difference, but, as many mentors and senior advisors have noted, this turned out to be a challenge.

For the first 5 years or so, I had two or three great associates working by my side, but I couldn't keep it interesting enough for them to stay on board with me. In retrospect, I didn't offer them enough upside to grow and generate their own business within a team format and compensate them accordingly. As a result, they decided to go off on their own and become a salesperson within our firm. I was happy for them at the time, but it was also a huge setback for me, as I had to retrain associates to take their place. Now, I allow my team members to grow and leverage our team platform so they can build their own book of business.

That started to change when James brought on a two associates simultaneously. Now the senior associate could train the junior. He started building a team based on roles that would support him and allow the team to better pursue and service its clients.

By the time he'd been in the business for 10 years, James, had a team of four. There was a full-time analyst and two entry-level associates. One of them was solely responsible for broker interactions, including listing agreements, transaction vouchers, deal memos, logging and the recording of the confidential agreements.

But James was still trying to manage all the listings himself. After all, he was a top producer and he figured he could handle the client contacts better than anyone on his team. That sounds logical, but it's a big mistake if you want to reap the rewards that come from a top performing team.

I call it the "Top Producer Trap." I'll let James describe how it looked for him.

The one thing that I never let go of was that client interaction, and I really, really spread myself thin. I was working around the clock—not that I'm afraid of hard work, but it just was not efficient.

You get maxed out. I've found that if you're doing the right job by your client and you're communicating with them regularly throughout the week, you really can't do that for more than 20 to 25 clients. And so I was out there trying to manage 40 or so listings. It was just not working.

Things started to slip through the cracks, and it was very frantic at times, because I really was still in control of all that. I mean, vacation? I had the cell phone tethered to me 24/7, because in most cases I was the only person who had the answers.

James says, "It's hard to believe that it took me close to 14–15 years to figure this out." In fact, it's fairly normal. First you have to become aware that what you've been doing isn't working anymore. Ideally, you would see the crises coming and make productive changes well before you have to. The reality is that most of us don't start looking for a new way to do things until we realize that the old way simply isn't working, or we understand that we can produce so much more with some very basic changes.

One reason we don't change is that little voice in our head that says, "You can do it faster and better, so you should do it." Besides, you've been successful so far, doing things that way, so it feels comfortable and right. I continually remind our own coaching clients a very simple, yet hard-to-accept truth: Just because you can do it faster and better doesn't mean it will make you wealthier.

You have to change your thinking from maximizing your production to maximizing the team's production. Your most important job as a team leader is to help the team succeed.

When James started to recognize the need to have his team members begin working directly with some of his clients and handle other opportunities, he also started on the road to a much more productive team.

He had to create a different team. Instead of arranging things so everyone supported him, James organized the team so it became more territorial and point-person focused. Some of the change almost happened naturally.

Mitch Levine joined James's team as an analyst in 2008. He started helping out more and more with clients and discovered that he was really good at it. Mitch started taking on more of the client reporting. It freed up a lot of James's time, and that made a huge difference.

I realized, wow, I don't have to be the day-to-day person. I need to know what's going on, but my senior team members can advise me. So we kind of figured out our pointe-person system, even though we only labeled it this the last year or two.

Today, every one of the team's listings has a point-person. James is never the sole point of contact with the client. Even when he is the primary contact, James makes sure there's another team member who knows what's going on.

That's better for the team. They can work more listings and work them effectively, which means more profit. Today they service about sixty listings, with each point-person responsible for approximately ten. That makes things better for their clients.

Clients don't experience a slowdown in the process just because James is out of the office. Recently, he took a three week business trip to China. With the 12-hour time difference and sketchy communications, he was simply out of touch for a lot of that time. His team members kept client projects moving. The new team organization gives clients other benefits, too.

Operating under Massey Knakal's unique "Territory System," James's associates know the buildings in their respective territories better than he does, so clients always get the best information. And having associates handle more listings frees James up to do what he thinks he does best: "originating business and then helping close it."

When you see the transition written out like this, it looks both easy and inevitable. It was neither. Changes in the way a team works and changes in personal attitudes and behavior are not easy. They require commitment and discipline, and even then they don't move smoothly. There's no guarantee of success. Everyone on the team needs to have the same vision. This can be challenging when several members of your team are independent contractors.

James faced the personal challenge of learning to be a team leader. The transition from individual contributor or producer to team leader is one of the hardest in business and life. James had to learn to step back from old habits and behaviors that had worked for years and try to do things a new way.

The team had to make changes, too. In many cases the change involves bringing new people on board, people who don't have to break old habits to do things the new way.

In 2010, 2 years after James saw the need to change things, the team was still only four people and a slightly improved version of how things had been before. That was when they hired Caroline Hannigan. Mitch Levine, James' Director of Sales, interviewed her first, and then she had an interview with James. She still remembers the first question he asked her.

"Where do you see yourself in 5 years?"

That's the kind of question you ask when you're thinking about a team growing and changing and you want people who can help make that happen. In the last 4 years, the team has doubled in size and Caroline has moved from associate to senior associate to sales team manager. The team has changed in other ways, too.

Hiring an analyst has freed up Mitch to spend more time on client work. Associates have assigned territories, and James has had to change his behavior to make it all work. It's been a learning experience for everyone, one that Caroline describes this way:

Originally, James was the one running every property. He liked being the one speaking with the client, which meant he had to know everything that was going on with the property. The last few years have been a learning experience for the whole team, James included. I don't want to say it was tough, but it definitely took some time for James to come around and listen to what team members were telling him, and loosen the reins.

Establishing the point-person role, and sticking to it, was our biggest advantage to how we've grown in the last 2 years. Team members are now running listings from start to finish, allowing James to grow as an agent and for the team to evolve.

In 2011, James completed 24 sales worth over $150 million. He won the company's Gerald W. Bridges Award as company-wide Salesperson of the Year. When the award was presented, James took his entire team with him to the front of the room to accept it, with this explanation.

The Salesperson of the Year award is not a personal award. The team atmosphere here is something I've definitely embraced. There's no way I could have handled the sales I did last year on my own.

James had embraced his role as team leader, but the adjustments were not done. As the team grew to a half dozen people, he found that he was putting more of his time into the day-to-day management of team activities. That would be good, except that it conflicted with his goal to spend as much time as possible originating and closing business.

His solution was to create a new position, sales team manager, to facilitate day-to-day team operations. James had already identified "strategic thinking" as one of Caroline's strengths, so she was the logical choice for the job. Her job is to make sure that the team gets the answers and support they need from the firm and to stay on top of the status of all the projects.

As James notes, the team is still a work in progress. Most teams are. But we can learn some lessons about top producing commercial real estate teams by digging into the details of how James Nelson's team gets the job done.

THE POINT-PERSON SYSTEM

James and his team developed their point-person system to work within Massey Knakal's territory approach. Each new listing was allocated to a single point-person on the team to service. However, James would also introduce the point-person to the client early on in the procurement process, so that he would not be seen as the go-to person for everyday tasks that normally arise in securing and servicing listings. Additionally, the reporting internally and externally became much more efficient.

The team is organized around the principle of building on strengths. The idea is to have everyone doing what they do best to contribute to team success. In James's case, that means organizing things so he can originate and execute more business and spend less time doing routine administrative work. In Caroline's case, that means creating a new position that contributes to team success and enables her to use her "strategic" strength. In other cases, like Mitch, it means shifting someone to a role that will contribute more to team production and finding someone else who can make the contribution he made before.

Here is an example of how a point-person may interact with the team when pursuing and securing an exclusive listing opportunity.

Opinion of Value (OV) Process:
1. JN gets an OV request.
2. Assign point-person.

3. CH emails MT and cc point-person so that MT can begin working on the OV.
4. Immediately, point-person works with JN (and MK agent is applicable) for any and all information needed for MT to do the OV.
5. All OVs are submitted to the point-person and MK agent (if applicable).
6. Final version of the OV then goes to JN.
7. Once OV is presented, email it to CH to log in our database and MKSS.

Process When Hired:
1. Point-person works with MT and WY to put together the marketing materials.
2. Point-person reaches out to client for items needed for materials/marketing.
3. CH will write an executive summary, if needed.
4. CH and point-person review brochure.
5. JN gives final look over, before sending it to client.

Point-Person Responsibilities:
- Go on pitch with JN, and handle 50% of presentation.
- Follow up with client and establish point-person as main point of contact ⋯⟩ cc JN.
- Work with MK agent (whether agent originates in our territory or we originate in their territory).
- Create call lists for property and delegate to team members.
- Conduct weekly follow-up with client via phone and email.
- Generate reports.
- Email team updates on property (how to respond to offers, highest offer, tours, etc.).
- Work with MT regarding any changes and updates needed to be made to marketing materials ⋯⟩ recirculate and repost.

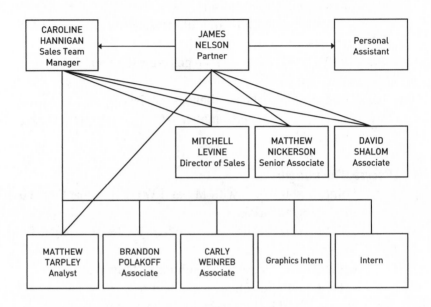

Team Nelson organizational chart

The principle of a point-person is simple, but it can be hard to put into practice. As teams grow in size, so does the challenge to balance people's preferences and strengths with the needs of the team. The main tool for harnessing team strengths and making them productive is the Team Operating Agreement.

TEAM OPERATING AGREEMENT

Unfortunately, but not surprisingly, most teams do not have a team vision statement. Most don't even have job descriptions. Team Nelson has both in place, but they also have a Team Operating Agreement.

The title is important. This is a team document. Every team member gets it, so he or she can see the team's goals, what's expected of them and also what's expected of other team members. And all team members sign it as a commitment to doing their part.

The team agreement includes general rules of conduct about how team members will deal with each other. A team vision outlines goals in general terms. The team agreement also includes a limited number of measurable team goals for the current year, as well as the processes for winning and fulfilling business and the responsibilities of a point-person.

The Team Operating Agreement includes a detailed description of the duties and responsibilities of every team member, but they're nothing like the standard job description. The individual sections are about specific behavior and performance standards.

Duties and responsibilities cover what a team member is expected to do. There's a description of how much work should be internal and how much should be outside the office and a listing of the important tasks the team member is responsible for.

The Team Operating Agreement also includes specific performance metrics for every team member. These can be things like how many of the team's listings they are expected to be the point-person for, how many calls they're expected to make, etc. The metrics do two important things.

First, clear, understood metrics for what's expected make it easy to evaluate performance and behavior. It's easy to assess whether a team member is spending time as planned, making the number of calls expected and more. The Team Operating Agreement also ensures the team vision is being met and the client's needs are being served.

There are outcome measures. Some of those measures tie directly to the Team Operating Agreement. And there are activity measures of how people are spending their time.

The Team Operating Agreement is the link between overall team goals and the duties and responsibilities of team members. That's only the first step in good performance management. A way to compare actual performance and behavior with the agreement has to be included, or the duties and responsibilities listed there are just hope. Procedures must be in place that link expectations to reality.

For a copy of the *Team Nelson's Team Operating Agreement,* please visit **www.massimo-group.com/TeamBook**. You will need the password "Nelson" (with a capital N) to access this document.

COMMUNICATION EQUALS SUCCESS

Every team needs to stay on track and keep moving forward to accomplish their goals. That happens through a combination of informal communication and formal process, and with Team Nelson it starts with how the office is arranged.

The team members sit in small open cubicles right next to one another, all at eye level with each other. The desks are connected, and everyone can hear what everyone else is doing. The way things are set up, James is surrounded by the team. They're so close that Caroline says that if one of them gets sick, they all get sick, but that kind of proximity also makes for good informal communication.

Every team needs good informal communications. Those are the unplanned conversations that happen naturally when people are together. Team Nelson's seating arrangements make that easy and effective.

Team members also have situational meetings between members. This kind of bullpen arrangement makes that easy, too. It's easy to grab another team member to discuss a specific issue, project or client.

The formal process of making the team successful starts with data. James says:

> We track everything. We track weekly goals. We track how many calls everyone makes. How many owner meetings. Networking events. How many referrals we send out. How many additions they made to our mailing list.

Caroline is responsible for making sure all that data comes together. When I interviewed her for the book, the phrase "I work with" sprang from her lips again and again. Caroline's title is "Sales Team *Manager*," and that's what she does. Whether it's documents or data, Caroline is the person responsible for keeping it moving so it gets to the person who needs it. It's also her job to make sure James knows what he needs to be the team leader.

Caroline and James meet every Thursday. At that meeting they make sure that things are updated. They review team progress and issues and make sure they have an updated listing report. They review goals every week, except for income, which James prefers to evaluate quarterly. In James's words, they "tee things up for the team meeting on Friday."

The whole team meets on Friday at 7:30 a.m. There was a time when the team meeting was mostly James talking, but that's changed, and it's a good example of how James and the team have evolved.

Now they go around the room and each point-person reports on his or her listings. It's also a time to discuss new ideas or the things the team should be working on. James expects everyone to know the basics of every listing, and this is where team members can ask specific questions.

The team has found that meeting at the end of the week works best for them. They've found that Friday is a good time to review the week's activities, and to see if they have achieved their weekly goals. On Monday, team members can hit the ground running, taking on whatever challenge they think is most important.

Caroline and James meet with every team member once a month. They go over that team member's leads, Top 100 contacts and point properties, and they discuss where James may be able to help them secure business. James has an open-door policy, and the office layout fosters informal meetings, so most issues are resolved on the fly. The monthly meeting is an opportunity to look at overall performance and discuss any open issues.

The monthly schedule seems to be about right. It includes time for significant progress between meetings, and informal meetings can handle questions as they come up. But a monthly cycle is still short enough that James can catch any serious issues early enough to deal with them effectively.

The Team Operating Agreement is important at this point. It also illustrates how James and the team have evolved.

James says he used to set goals for team members. If they hit those goals, great, but sometimes they didn't. When that happened, the team member could always claim that the goals were unreasonable. No more. Having the team member sign off on his or her own goals takes a lot of wiggle room out of the discussions on performance.

This is a high-performance culture. The people who thrive here are hard workers who are willing to commit to their goals and then be accountable for their performance.

FINDING AND KEEPING WINNERS

James lives in Connecticut, but he still gets to his Manhattan office around 6:45 in the morning. When he does, half the team is already there. He has no idea when they get in. That's just part of a high-performance team culture. James thinks it starts with hiring leaders.

He gives a lot of credit for his team culture to Massey Knakal's founders. He says the firm looks for leaders. College credentials and GPA are important, of course, but they look for evidence of the intangible "right stuff" that makes a winner.

They're looking for people who will commit to something and are successful. James uses himself as an example. He jokes that he was lucky Massey Knakal didn't require a cover letter when he applied, because he didn't have one. He certainly hadn't dreamed about commercial real estate as his life's work. James is sure that his most important credential was the fact that he was the captain of a Division I swim team.

Once you've hired top people and done the hard work of training them and integrating them into the team, you want them to stay as long as possible. In general, people's value increases the longer they stay with the team and keep growing.

They increase their knowledge of the territory and the nuances of the business. They develop relationships with clients and broaden their referral network. James thinks one of the things he has going for him is the team itself:

> Some people will always want to go off and do their thing. Some people just say, "Look, I want to do it on my own." Some of my team members could absolutely go out on their own and be very successful. But I think my team members have realized the benefits of leveraging the team's platform.

The team offers an associate reputation, experience and expertise they can't duplicate on their own. That means they can simply be more successful as part of the team than they might be alone. They can excel at what they're best at, leverage the team platform and be financially rewarded for it.

James also works on the team culture. Team members spend a lot of time together. The basic rules for interaction are outlined in the Team Operating Agreement and reinforced in both casual interactions and one-to-one meetings. Then there are events designed to foster team spirit and togetherness.

Some are formal team-building events, with the clear business purpose of teaching the team to work better together. One was a regatta-style event where the team learned to row a racing shell. There are regular events, like the annual Secret Santa luncheon at a fine restaurant and occasional outings such as a ski weekend.

Finding, training and retaining winners is one of the biggest challenges you will face as a team leader. One of your challenges is making sure that compensation is a reason people want to stay with you.

TEAM COMPENSATION

Compensation also helps foster longevity. James wants his top associates to make as much as the top people at the company. They get a base salary plus a percentage of the team's net and an additional bonus when they bring in business. The compensation and responsibilities of the team are as follows:

Mitchell Levine—Director of Sales
- Salary plus percentage of team commissions
- Runs listings as an executor and originates business in his sub-territory.

Caroline Hannigan—Sales Team Manager
- Salary plus percentage of team commissions
- Conducts day-to-day operations and oversees team procedures. Additionally, she also handles James's secondary email account, works with PR & Marketing to develop press and marketing materials, sets up team email blasts, tracks referrals, assigns and handles the listing pipeline, tracks and vouchers transactions, creates listing agreements and transaction memos, creates and tracks invoices, assists in creating the monthly Nelson Report e-newsletter and reviews and proofs all articles and materials produced by the team. She is also responsible for running listings as an executor.

Matthew Nickerson—Senior Associate
- Salary plus percentage of team commissions
- Runs listings as an executor and originates business in his sub-territory. Additionally, he tracks all 1031 buyers and creates and logs confidentiality agreements.

David Shalom—Associate
- Salary plus percentage of team commissions
- Runs listings as an executor and originates business in his sub-territory.

Brandon Polakoff—Associate
- Salary
- Assists with tours of properties, makes investor calls on the team's properties, and reaches out to the brokerage community. Additionally, he assists the team manager with tracking statistics, handles James's social media accounts, assists the team's analyst on OVs and research and updates the team on the outside broker listings in our territory and

our weekly targeted phone calls.

Matthew Tarpley—Analyst
- Salary plus percentage of team commissions
- Produces all property valuations for the team and assists in creating marketing materials. He also logs all property transfers, creates territory comps, posts all new listings to the online MLS and produces monthly team market share report. Additionally, he runs a few listings as an executor.

Carly Weinreb—Associate
- Salary
- Schedules and gives tours of properties, logs offers and tours, makes investor calls on the team's properties, and reaches out to the brokerage community. Additionally, she handles updating the weekly reports for the team's clients and creates the monthly Nelson Report e-newsletter and monthly listing packet.

Graphic Designer
- Hourly
- Creates all marketing materials.

Intern
- Hourly
- Supports associates on day-to-day projects, keeps the team's property brochure shelf stocked, updates the list of monthly listings and maintains the team REA database.

Intern
- Hourly
- Supports associates on day-to-day projects, inputs new additions into REA and manages James's contact list.

Personal Assistant
- Salary
- Handles all of James's personal matters and his work schedule.

GETTING THE MOST FROM YOUR DAY

One objective of the point-person system is to arrange things so James can do what he does best and what makes the biggest contribution to the team: originating and closing business. Any minute that James spends doing internal work in the office is a minute that isn't devoted to his primary focus.

We've seen how a combination of team structure and letting go of some work makes it possible for James to meet the challenge. But there's also the important component of time management. What can he do to maximize the amount of time he devotes to originating and closing business?

Taking control of his time starts early. James is on the 5:50 a.m. train from Connecticut to Manhattan. The train is less crowded than it will be later in the morning, so James can get a seat and work on answering emails and other paperwork.

His day may include a scheduled meeting with Caroline, the entire team or individual team members. The rest of the day should be devoted to spending as much time as possible on outside work while still functioning as an effective team leader.

As team leader, James is expected to support his team members. He has an open-door policy and will always make time to speak with one of them. That's important work, but he has to monitor the time he spends on it. The open office sometimes makes that harder. I'll let him describe the situation:

> I still really struggle to get my calls in because every time I get off the phone there are usually two or three people who have a question for me. We try to keep sacred call hours, so I try to say, "Look, guys I'm doing my calls. Talk to me later in the day. Or hey, grab me before 9 a.m."

James used to answer his own phones or screen calls with caller ID. He quickly learned this was an unnecessary step that took up a lot of time and wasn't the best for customer service. Now his sales team manager answers his line and then forwards the call to the appropriate team member handling the assignment. This way, James has more time for calls with his top clients and prospects.

Dealing with interruptions and questions is a constant challenge. James has been known to take a stopwatch to the office to track time he spends on internal work. This is a simple exercise his coach had him do, but it helps him understand how he is really spending his day. On one occasion, James found that he was spending 2½ hours a day on non-revenue-generating activities.

The time that James isn't originating or closing business isn't all time spent talking to team members. It might be reviewing documents. There's time spent to meet his obligations to the firm. All these activities are important. But team leaders must constantly strive for the right balance between internal and external work.

James has two people who really help him be more efficient. He has a personal assistant who handles personal matters like phone bills and balancing the checkbook and a host of business matters. Scheduling is one of the most important. Think about it. If you want to schedule a conference call with five other busy people, it can occupy you for days. There will likely be dozens of emails back and forth and more than a couple of calls before the appointment is set. When James faces that problem, he delegates it to his personal assistant. She also handles registration for events.

James also has a driver. Right now you may be rolling your eyes and thinking, "That's just a self-indulgent luxury." It isn't. Remember New York City expands across five boroughs, and Team Nelson has clients in all five as well as in Westchester County and New Jersey.

Before the driver, James did what most people do: He'd take cabs. If you've ever been to any big city, especially New York, you know how crazy that can be. The stress level goes way up, you wind up late for some meetings, and cabs often aren't the place to get some work done while you travel. Plus, cabs are not cheap. Those problems go away when you have a car and driver. That's a big benefit for James in terms of productivity and stress reduction, but there's more.

I share my driver with the team. I tell them that is this is just not our personal driver, this is really a benefit for the client. Anytime we can send the car out to pick up a client and show him or her around town, that's really a nice touch. And if I have a client who's going uptown and I'm going downtown, guess what? I'm hopping out. I'm taking the cab. The client is going uptown because first and foremost it's a really nice feature to be able to offer to the client.

James takes the train into the city in the morning, but he uses the driver for his commute home at the end of the day. That way he's not tied to train schedules and he can do some work on the drive. The evening trains are crowded, and it's impossible to make calls or get serious work done.

———————◆———————

Understanding the value of your time and delegating less productive tasks to other team members is an essential part of keeping the team moving forward. Do you know what your time is worth? To access a quick exercise and calculate *Your Hourly and Daily Worth*, please visit **www.massimo-group.com/TeamBook**. The password to access this content is "Time" (with a capital T).

———————◆———————

I think this is impressive, but don't make the mistake of thinking that it's either perfect or that things will stay the way they are forever. There will be changes to the team that will mean changes in the way work gets done. And there will always be ways to do things better.

The team and James's personal time management have come a long way in the last few years. He's far more productive and efficient than he was, but he's still looking for ways to do things even more effectively and get more phone time and more time to work with clients.

IN THEIR OWN WORDS

I asked Caroline and James each to share one piece of advice about how to have a successful team.

Caroline Hannigan—Sales Team Manager

You won't have a perfect team even if you have all the

MVPs. You have to know the roles you're looking to fill in order to have that successful team; then you need to look for the people with the right traits and attributes to fill those roles.

Not everyone here wants to be a broker like James. We want to be part of a team that works together to achieve the same goal. We are all competitive individuals who bring something different to the table. I think we want to be with people who will push us to be better.

Everyone is looking to be successful. So I'd say surround yourself with the right group of people. Always look to do better. Be competitive. It's an eat-what-you-kill industry. And if you don't want to do that, then you should find something else.

James Nelson

Team responsibilities and goals should be clearly established from the start, ensuring that all aspects of the brokerage business are accounted for. Every team member should focus in on what they do best to add the most value. Activities should be streamlined and delegated accordingly. Time is the most valuable asset that we all have in this business, so every minute you spend you have to ask yourself, "Is this the most productive thing I can be doing now?" both for your business and clients.

The experience of Team Nelson can teach us a lot, but I believe there are three big lessons. First, in some other teams we profiled, the principals planned a lot before they created their team. Team Nelson evolved to more of an integrated team, while continuing to do business and be successful. Second, if you're thinking about making your team more integrated, you should study this chapter. Team Nelson has a formal Team Operating Agreement that lays out the way the team will work and describes the important cultural values. Third, and maybe most important, leading a team is a particular role, and most people have to learn the job on the fly.

NEXT UP

The next chapter is about a team that is almost the opposite of Team Nelson. They don't have a Team Operating Agreement or formal procedures. Heck, they don't even have a regular review meeting. Instead, they depend on excellent fit between their personalities and tons of informal communication to drive their success.

MASON RETAIL GROUP

"My Way"

Team Size: 4
Markets: Nationwide
Focus: Specialty Retail

Jeff Mason does things his own way. His firm, Mason Retail Group (MRG), is a consultancy, not a traditional brokerage. He got where he is today by a very unconventional route, and his team and the way they work is different, too. It's been like that since Jeff left college and went into the corporate world.

He joined a company called Merry Go Round Enterprises, which was "a junior fashion apparel mall-based specialty retail chain." He stayed there for 9 years, helping the chain grow to over a thousand stores.

Next, Jeff moved to a company called Garden Botanica. At the time, they were funded by private equity firms, and they went public in 1996. In 1997, Jeff moved on to his next challenge.

He joined the specialty retail consulting firm of Gray & Associates, based in Portland, Oregon. Jeff opened the East Coast office. However, like most team leaders, he grew tired of a compensation ceiling and wanted the opportunity enjoy all the benefits of his hard work. There were very few consulting companies back then, and the playing field was wide open. In January 2000 he founded Mason Retail Group. The firm contractually represents specialty retail tenants and specialty shopping venues. Jeff had always been entrepreneurial, and after 12-plus years in a corporate environment he was ready to control his own destiny.

Mason Retail Group is a consulting firm, which means they do things differently from a commercial brokerage and commission based, financing firms. One big difference is compensation. Deal making team members receive a salary and bonus because Jeff thinks that "incentivizes them the right way" to develop the kind of business relationships a consulting firm needs. Bonuses are based on individual performance and overall company success on an annual basis.

Jeff's relationships gave him a bit of a head start in business because a handful of his clients followed him to his new firm. Even so, it was a lean start. In the beginning, Mason Retail Group was just Jeff and a phone and a lot of connections. There was also a problem.

Jeff is an awful typist, so hiring an assistant was a priority. If you believe you are completely self-sufficient administratively, you are wrong. Jeff thinks that making an administrative assistant your first hire is a no-brainer.

One of my favorite speakers is Nido Quebin. If you don't know who he is, Google him; it will be well worth your time. One of Nido's quotes is "To do is transactional. To stop doing, your stop doing list leads you to your list called to be. I must be before I can do." Sounds pretty heavy, but it is so simple. Just focusing on transactions will unfortunately put you on the "Transaction Treadmill." You may be getting deals done, but your business really isn't growing or moving ahead. Jeff, like all great team leaders, simply recognized that he wasn't moving forward by typing, or performing several other tasks. He created a Not to Do list and built his team around what he wanted *to be.*

———————•———————

Regardless of your role on your team, you know there are certain things you continue to do that you should. It's time to get off the "Transaction Treadmill." To download your own copy of a *Not To Do List*, please visit **www.massimo-group.com/TeamBook**. You will need the password "NotToDo" to access this document.

———————•———————

In addition to typing, the assistant handled paperwork and telephone answering, things that Jeff would have to do otherwise. That freed up his time to concentrate on making deals.

Kevin Kohnen joined the team in the summer of 2001. Kevin and Jeff have known each other since Kevin was 10 because Jeff's wife is Kevin's cousin. Jeff unwittingly hired him right out of college.

Even though they'd known each other a long time, Kevin really didn't know what Jeff's business was until Jeff and his wife, Nancy, invited Kevin and his girlfriend for the weekend after Thanksgiving in 2000. Here's how Kevin tells that story of getting hired:

> I have known Jeff since I was shooting jump shots with him in the backyard up at the family cabin. I actually offered myself a job through multiple cocktails. Jeff and I were talking, and he said "Someday it would be great if you could work with me. I think it would really be a home run." And so, at 21 years old, I took that as "Hey, this is great. I have got a job."
>
> I went back home and I was energized and told my mother that Jeff offered me a job. Well, she called Jeff's wife, Nancy, and said, "Isn't it great that Jeff offered Kevin a job?"
>
> Nancy hung up the phone, ran into the kitchen and questioned Jeff about this unexpected turn of events. Obviously I had misunderstood, and Jeff hadn't actually offered me a job, or at least he didn't think he had. As always, Jeff turned an extreme negative into what was a positive. He turned it around and said, "Why wouldn't I hire him? I have known him all my life. There is no background check necessary. I know what type of person he is." And that is how I ended up at Mason Retail Group.

That story tells you a lot about how Jeff does things. He trusts his gut. And he has a great personality, something that helps him turn negatives into positives and build strong relationships.

Until 2004, the firm was Jeff, Kevin, and an administrative assistant. Then there were a lot of changes.

The company was growing rapidly, and Jeff and Kevin were having trouble keeping up with the work. Jeff went looking for a person with the right personality and skill set to be a deal maker. He "networked around" for several months until he found his second associate, who was then working at The Rouse Company.

The firm kept growing. The next deal maker that Jeff brought on board was a college friend of Kevin who was working selling furniture for one of Jeff's friends.

By that time, Kevin was experienced enough to help train new people, and Mason Retail Group had a solid team. Jeff's wife, Nancy, had her own consulting firm, specializing in the landlord side of the business. When Jeff and Nancy had twins in 2004, they merged her firm into the Mason Retail Group. Now the combined firm was doing both retail representation and landlord representation.

In 2006, the administrative assistant left and they had to hire another one. This time, Jeff took Nancy's suggestion and used an employment agency. Nancy and one of the associates did most of the interviewing as a team. They reduced the number of candidates to two for Jeff to interview. After he did, they all voted to hire Pat West. A common thread among dominant teams is the application of a formal hiring process.

Pat could type, as she says, "with the best of them," but otherwise she isn't much like what you'd expect for an assistant in a specialty retail firm. Before MRG she'd been a steelworker and had worked in an attorney's office. She didn't know the business at all, even using the wrong spelling for "site" in the first email she ever typed for Jeff.

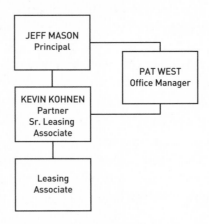

Mason Retail Group organizational chart

That would have put off some people, but Jeff's philosophy is that you hire people who you think will fit into the team. Fit is the most important thing. Jeff thinks that if he has a person who fits in, he can work with them to develop the skills they need.

Before the recession took hold, MRG had grown to four deal makers, with Pat to support them. But as was true of many other firms, the recession changed the game. The fortunes of Jeff's firm were linked to the fortunes of the specialty retail industry.

When retailers do well, they grow. When they do poorly, they don't. In the recession, the retail chains cut back severely on their growth plans. That made it hard for the Mason Retail Group. Here's how Jeff describes it:

> In the recession, the opportunities really dwindled. And so we didn't need to think about growing. We thought about survival in 2009 and 2010. I just took a conservative approach and decided not to grow, not to bring someone on, until I was relatively sure that we could keep them and keep them busy and keep them active.

That time came in late 2013. Business had been picking up and Jeff and Kevin were struggling to keep up again. Jeff's second associate had left the business to stay home with her children. Kevin's friend had moved to a corporate job. They needed another deal maker.

In January of 2014, they hired new associate, Alex Gaines. In his first year, his primary responsibility is marketing and leasing the new ground-up, mixed-use development in Chattanooga, Tennessee, The Village at Waterside. Kevin is now a partner and he has taken the lead role in training Alex.

Jeff is already thinking ahead. He expects growth to continue and he "has a couple of other people in mind for the next positions."

HIRING

In my career, I've identified two approaches to internal growth. Some firms recruit today for where they want to be tomorrow. They bring on team members before they really need them so that when they do, the new team member will be up to speed.

Other firms try to handle as much as they can with the current team and only hire someone new when the workload is uncomfortable. That's Jeff's approach, especially after the recession. Now, he's much more cautious about bringing people on board with the idea that the business will come.

That doesn't mean that Jeff doesn't think ahead about staffing. He's identified things that might happen that would require MRG to add more deal makers. He's just not ready to pull the trigger yet.

Jeff usually hires people he already knows or who come to him through some kind of referral. Other firms usually spend most of their recruiting effort and energy on vetting candidates during the hiring process. Jeff spends time well before the first formal contact, evaluating whether the person he's spotted has the skills, style and values to be a productive team member.

He can hire that way because he wants people who fit his team and who don't know anything about the business. Here's his hiring perspective in a nutshell:

> My philosophy when hiring a new dealmaker is to search for a young, raw talent who has the necessary attributes for success as a retail real estate consultant. I look for a strong work ethic, great personality, and good moral fiber. When I find the right candidate, they join the company with no experience in the industry. They are taught the right way do to business from the very beginning. For example, when I was looking for a new associate, I reached out to several old friends at my high school, Boy's Latin, and asked them to think about a person who embodied the qualities I was looking for. I gave them specific traits and they recommended Alex. Kevin and I then had multiple lunches with Alex to get to know him and determine if we felt he would be a good fit for the team.

Naturally, that means the new person won't be productive right away. Jeff says there's a 2-year learning curve. He puts people to work immediately so they're helping to move deals forward from the beginning, but with a lot of guidance and assistance. There's no formal training program, but the way Jeff does things looks very much like an apprentice program.

The new person starts by doing support tasks and listening to how Jeff and Kevin work. He or she goes along on trips, which expose them to the business and the clients, and which also function as training. After a while, he or she starts to handle some things personally, with support from Jeff and Kevin. Eventually the new person is handling his or her own deals.

This is a very personal kind of training. There is no set curriculum. Instead, the new person learns from watching and listening and asking questions. The more experienced people explain what they're doing when necessary or when asked. It also relies on the learner's having a strong work ethic and letting people know when help is needed.

Jeff thinks through the best way to do something, based on his experience and values. Then he does what he thinks is right. That starts with the way he gets new business.

LETTING THE GAME COME TO JEFF

Successful brokerage teams always have a clearly defined way to market their services to potential clients. Most consulting firms have a business development plan. Jeff's plan at Mason Retail Group is to let the business come to them.

All their business on both the tenant and the landlord side comes through referral. I pressed Jeff about that, because in my experience, if you don't market, you die. Here's how Jeff explained the dynamics of his business:

> You walk in and say, "Hi, I am Jeff Mason. I think you have a neat concept. I would like to help you grow." People are very skeptical about that, and it just doesn't work.

Mason Retail Group works with specialty retail clients to help them implement their strategic growth plan. There's a saying that retail is all about location. You can have the best concept in the world, but if you don't have stores in the right places, you'll still have the concept but you won't have a growing business. MRG's job is to help the growth happen.

That means helping retailer clients like Arhaus Furniture find locations that fit their concept so they can grow the business. On the landlord side, it means helping venues attract the best specialty fashion retailers, restaurants and entertainment concepts. Other major clients of MRG are Under Armour, Harbor East in Baltimore and The Village of Waterside.

So how do these potential clients find MRG? They ask around. Jeff has been in the business now for almost 30 years. He knows a lot of people, and so does Kevin. And a lot of people know them and the kind of work they do.

Jeff is a personable guy and people like him, but that's not enough to make the phone ring. The firm has an excellent reputation. Retailers know them and the quality of work they do. Retail executives move between companies and take their knowledge of Mason Retail Group with them.

The reason Jeff can rely solely on referral business is that he's invested 30 years in reputation and relationship building. He also puts relationships at the forefront of the way he deals with clients, including the way the firm assigns work. He has neither the desire nor the need to grow MRG into a large consulting firm. His way works, both professionally and personally.

GETTING THE WORK DONE

In most brokerages, the work is divided up based on geographical territory or specialty or some combination of the two. At the Mason Retail Group, work is doled out based on "who has the most positive relationship to get the job done."

That sounds simple, but it takes a lot of work. But Jeff tries to get everyone involved in every project. No team member specializes in any one kind of work. Every team member is a generalist, and he or she is also expected to work on every project. Getting everyone involved in every project means that one person can step in for another if that's what's needed. Here's an example.

Taubman Centers is a publicly traded company that owns regional shopping malls in the United States, where they have the highest retail sales per square foot of any similar company. Jeff spent 4 years working with them to find the right opportunities to bring Arhaus Furniture to their portfolio of shopping malls.

Both parties finally settled on University Town Center in Sarasota, Florida. Over the next 6 months, Jeff negotiated the deal and got it approved by both companies. A letter of intent was finalized and the lease was drafted. Jeff also worked on a deal at International Plaza in Tampa, Florida, but that is still a work in progress.

Taubman set a deadline for lease execution that created a situation that might have posed a problem in some other firms. Jeff had already booked a vacation in Ireland for the week leading up to the deadline. Jeff went off on vacation, and Kevin stepped in to negotiate the leases.

That wasn't a problem because Kevin knew the deal structure intimately. He knew each transaction and the nuances of each deal because there is constant communication between team members so that everyone knows what everyone else is working on.

This team is different from the individual specialists, or the integrated teams we have studied in this book. There is no one "right" structure to success.

Constant communication starts with the office environment. The team works in an open environment with partial walls. Everyone can hear everyone else. Pat says that can be confusing, but she uses it to her advantage. When she hears Jeff talking about something that she knows will result in an email, she can jump the gun and get started on it, before he asks. When you get to this point, you know you have the right assistant!

Outside the office, constant communication is conversation. That happens on trips, when two of the deal makers go out of town together and have plenty of time to talk. It also happens on shorter trips where two of them spend half an hour or so in the car. Jeff and Kevin have a family connection, so they talk when they see each other at family events or on the weekend.

The iPads that everyone has carry a lot of the communication load. Emails and shared files can let others know how a meeting went, share an idea, or ask for help. The phone is important, too. What's interesting are the two things that most teams use to communicate and keep people on the same page, but which don't have the same importance at MRG.

Most teams today use some kind of computerized CRM system as a key coordination tool. But MRG is much more paper-based than most brokerages.

Key documents are saved on the computer, of course. But when the firm completes a deal, it is edited down to the key pieces and saved as a paper file. That's the file that Jeff goes to when he wants to recall details of a deal that may have been done several years ago.

Meetings are another way that Mason Retail Group works differently from most brokerages. Most of the teams in this book use regular meetings as a way to coordinate and optimize their efforts and to set a cadence for the business. There are usually regular, weekly team meetings and regular one-on-one meetings in addition to project meetings. At MRG, there are only project meetings.

Jeff's thinking is that their constant communication is the way that they coordinate their efforts. In his words, "We don't do weekly catch-ups because we talk all the time."

But there are some situations where the best thing to do is get everyone together and have a meeting. Jeff shares an example:

> If we are doing a merchandising plan for a new retail project that we are working on, we all need to be at the office, sit down and go through it. We cut up the leasing plan, talk about the appropriate tenants that are right for each space, and more. You can only do that live with each other.

The way the Mason Retail Group handles meetings is only one aspect of their unique culture. Kevin described it succinctly as "Work hard and be nice to people."

Jeff Mason took his own unique path to his own unique niche. He chose what to do based on his passion for helping specialty retailers implement their strategic growth plan. Then he grew a team around him based on the way he thinks things should be done.

He hires people based on how well they will fit the team because he thinks that a productive and harmonious team is the best way to do great work for clients and enjoy the process. He hires people who don't know anything about the business because he wants to train them the right way and he's willing to take a couple of years for that.

Other teams have formal marketing plans and actively seek clients. Jeff lets the clients find him. People are assigned to lead projects based on their relationship with the client because Jeff thinks that's most likely to be effective in an environment where complex, multi-year projects are normal.

The result is a team that reflects Jeff's personality and approach to life and work. They work hard, they're productive, they communicate constantly and they get along very well.

Jeff says that you have a great team when "Everyone is pulling in the same direction with a smile on their face." If that's the test, then the Mason Retail Group is a great team.

IN THEIR OWN WORDS

Jeff Mason

> We enjoy what we do every day. And we enjoy doing it together because we are all pulling in the same direction. Everyone was carefully selected to be part of this team. And there is a similar quality in each of us that enables us to work efficiently and effectively together and enjoy the ride. Primarily, day in and day out, that's what we do. Everyone has a bump in the road every now and again because that's just the way life is, but to me that's what makes it interesting. It's certainly what makes our team successful and I would argue would make most teams successful.

Kevin Kohnen

> You have to have a great leader. If you don't respect that person and know that they are putting their absolute, 100% energy into it, day in and day out, you're going to go somewhere else if you're good enough. I do think to create a team, a bunch

of leaders and smart guys and girls who can figure it out, you have got to have someone to follow who you are willing to go to battle with. I think that is the key. That is the absolute key.

Pat West

Jeff and Kevin, their personalities absolutely go excellently together. I have seen them interact with people. I have never, ever heard Jeff raise his voice in the 8½ years I have been here. They both are very even-keeled, even-tempered people. They are patient, very patient because these deals, they do take weeks and weeks and months and sometimes years. Jeff just keeps at it. Kevin keeps at it. They are both very intelligent men. And I love working with them.

One important lesson from the Mason Retail Group is that what makes a good team depends on the circumstances. The team succeeds with a lot of informal communication and project meetings, instead of formal structures and processes, but that's partially a function of size. They're able to market the way they do because Jeff and the firm have an excellent reputation that's been growing for 30 years. A key lesson here is that your environment and market won't determine whether you can be successful with a team, but they will affect the kind of team that will get the best results.

NEXT UP

The environment plays a role for our next team, too. Our next team is part of larger firm that provides many resources they utilize to serve their clients. It's enabled them to build a solid team business based on strategic relationship building.

ASHLEY-HOLLIS

Long Term, Low Pressure

Team Size: 4
Market: Atlanta, Georgia
Focus: Tenant Representation

Ken Ashley and Sam Hollis have been have been working together in partnership for 18 years. In a business where many brokers are frantically chasing the next deal, they've worked out a more low-key way to be very successful. It involves a very disciplined and effective relationship management campaign and a comprehensive social media strategy, along with attention to and execution on all the brokerage basics. The next deal will always be there, but focusing on the success of relationships supported by excellence in execution has been their hallmark.

Sam was in the business first. He started out in Memphis, Tennessee, his home town, but moved to Atlanta, Georgia in 1987.

He worked as a junior to a senior broker who was a strong people person. Sam learned that what he himself brought to the table was detail and a numbers orientation that helped get transactions done. After 5 years, his senior left to start his own firm, and the pattern repeated.

This time Sam worked with another broker he describes as "relationship oriented." Once more Sam was the details-and-numbers guy. The two of them were doing one-off tenant work around Atlanta and decided they needed to add someone else who would go out and "kick up" business. Ken Ashley turned out to be that guy.

Ken started out his brokerage career focusing on leasing industrial properties, but after a couple of years he thought there was a lot more opportunity in office, given his personal network. He made the switch with the help of his mentor, Mark Christopher.

Mark taught Ken two important lessons. The first was that you have to "know your craft." He set Ken to reading leases on the weekends and taught him to analyze markets. Top performers and top teams become experts at what Ken calls their "craft." That takes hard work, and it takes discipline. Much of the expertise that brokers develop is not taught in school, so apprenticing under a great broker can really accelerate success, as would leveraging a mentor or even a coach.

The second lesson was that commercial real estate is about "friends and relationships." Most commercial real estate professionals I interact with tell me they're "client focused," even though many are really focused on the deal or the commission. Even among truly client-focused brokers and teams, very few have built their business on relationships that transcend the workplace. Ken says:

> Caring deeply about the individuals you work with and their own personal success is critical," says Ken. "Real estate will get you to the party, but everyone has a career and aspirations. "Enabling others to be successful first will translate to your own personal success in the end.

Tragically, after a courageous battle with cancer, Mark passed away. Ken realized he needed to figure out what to do next. He was still relatively new to the business, so he wanted to connect with someone who had more transaction experience and what he calls "deal wisdom." Sam seemed like someone who could help him figure out what would make the client happy and also "keep me out of trouble," Ken told me with a smile.

For his part, Sam thought Ken had skills that complemented his own. Ken wanted to go out and call on people; he liked that part of the business. And Sam thought Ken had excellent communications skills. When their other partner left for a different firm, they became a team unto themselves.

At first, they were an "informal team." It took them 9 months or so to decide to make their partnership formal. After that, it took a few years to, as Ken says, "true up" the relationship. For 15 years now, everything has been 50/50. There have been some other changes, though.

Until recently, the team has been Sam and Ken as principals and one or two junior brokers, supported by the Cushman & Wakefield administrative pool. Since 2005, four people have joined the team, learned something of the craft of commercial brokerage and then "spread their wings" and moved on.

That's a familiar pattern and it bothers some brokers. They feel like they train people new to the business only to have them leave just as they're becoming really productive. It doesn't bother Sam and Ken at all.

They're proud to have alumni who have all gone on to do other things at their firm or other places. Sam says:

> Just as we care about our clients, we really believe in our team. We expect people to work hard for our team, but they may have other opportunities arise. It's a small world, and you never know where people will end up. Former team members could well be a client in the future, but at a minimum we have a combined legacy going forward.

But in 2013, they changed their team in an important way by bringing Whitney Hembree on board.

———————————

For a copy of the Ashley-Hollis *New Member Onboarding Plan*, please visit **www.massimo-group.com/TeamBook**. You will need the password "Hollis" (with a capital H) to access this document.

———————————

Officially, Whitney's job title is brokerage coordinator, but in conversation, both Sam and Ken call the job "client coordinator." Whitney sees it as a kind of COO job, "keeping the team organized."

The work includes marketing, event planning, revenue tracking, organizing the prospecting and making sure that the deals are handled.

Whitney is a good fit with Sam and Ken for several reasons. She has experience in property management, which helped her understand commercial real estate. She's completed her MBA, which gives her a rich skill set and demonstrates that she has the kind of discipline the team was looking for.

Those are the kind of things you can pull off a résumé. Sam and Ken also describe other things that aren't as easy to describe precisely. They say she has "a winning way with people" and a "soft approach." They like the way she stays calm when the pressure's on. They know they can trust her.

That creates a very different kind of team. Whitney's job isn't to learn how to do the same things that Sam and Ken do. Her job is designed to help Sam and Ken do more of what they do well and make them more effective. They may be happy with junior brokers' learning the trade and then moving on, but with Whitney, it's different. As Sam says, only partly in jest, "Whitney can't leave." This is also consistent with their long-term, low pressure approach.

As of this writing, the team has hired an ambitious young man, William Linginfelter, to join the team when he graduates with a real estate degree from the University of Georgia. They're cautious, because they know about the investment they will need to make, in both time and money, in onboarding a new team member. However, after an extensive interview process, William took a personality profile, the AVA assessment mentioned earlier in this book. He matched the desired indicators, for the role he will play with this team, with flying colors. Williams's future appears to be very bright.

By the way, they don't subscribe to the idea that many brokerages and other businesses have, that "bigger is better." But there's another danger that worries them even more. Ken puts it this way:

> The danger of becoming a larger team is that you move away from your client-center focus and more into a management focus. We really love our clients and transacting business, so we'll leave the business of running the company to someone else.

That's really important because this team has built its business and long term success on their relationships with those clients.

I originally met Ken and Sam when they reached out to me regarding evaluating their team. Another common trait among dominant teams is that they are never satisfied and are always looking for improvement. Once I met Ken and Sam, I knew they had a story that needed to be shared. To learn how we worked with this top team and how they are enhancing their already impressive results, please see the *Ashley-Hollis Success Story* at **www.massimo-group.com/TeamBook**. You will need the password "Results" (with a capital R) to access this document.

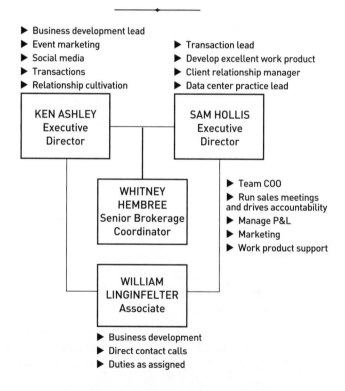

▶ Business development lead
▶ Event marketing
▶ Social media
▶ Transactions
▶ Relationship cultivation

▶ Transaction lead
▶ Develop excellent work product
▶ Client relationship manager
▶ Data center practice lead

KEN ASHLEY
Executive
Director

SAM HOLLIS
Executive
Director

WHITNEY HEMBREE
Senior Brokerage Coordinator

▶ Team COO
▶ Run sales meetings and drives accountability
▶ Manage P&L
▶ Marketing
▶ Work product support

WILLIAM LINGINFELTER
Associate

▶ Business development
▶ Direct contact calls
▶ Duties as assigned

Ashley-Hollis organizational chart

BUILDING A BUSINESS ON RELATIONSHIPS

Every team has to have an answer to the question, "Why should I do business with you?" I asked Ken how their team answers it. He told me that there are two things that set the team apart. Here's how he describes one of them:

> There are plenty of people who understand sticks and bricks and rates in this business. Unfortunately, that's not a differentiator. What makes us different is that we think about the why.
>
> We think about why we are even doing this project, and then what success looks like, well before we think about location issues and the landlord or the rate or any other details of the transaction. In other words, we think about the business strategy our client is about to undertake before we worry about the real estate deal.
>
> Many times what we're doing is helping a CEO or other high level executive fulfill the dream of what they want their company to be.

You can't develop a deep understanding of those dreams in a couple of meetings. You have to get to know the companies and the players, and that takes time. To use that time effectively, you have to be disciplined about who you want to work with.

Sam and Ken choose to work in what they call "the mid-cap space." They define that as companies with revenues between $200 million and $2 billion. Over the years, they've developed relationships with companies who meet the revenue test and who are "brand aware."

A brand-aware company is one that's aware of both its culture and the way they want to present their brand. That awareness influences all their decisions, including the ones they make about real estate. Porsche is a good example.

Ken developed and maintained a relationship and worked on smaller deals with Porsche Cars North America for more than a decade before the opportunity came along to handle the company's build-to-suit North American headquarters of 200,000 square feet on 56 acres adjacent to the Atlanta airport. The veritable mecca for Porsche enthusiasts will include a much vaunted "customer experience center" where current and aspiring owners can drive Porsche product on a handling circuit. The circuit includes a number of "destabilizing elements" like simulated ice hills and skid pans. Sam got involved to help coordinate the very complex transaction with a highly sophisticated client. The Atlanta Business Chronicle named it the Deal of the Year for 2011. The team also completed a mirror of the Atlanta Porsche transaction in Los Angeles in 2012, sans the headquarters.

I think there are two different views of the Ashley-Hollis team. From 30,000 feet you can see the patient relationship building that happens over the long term. But from ground level, the team works like many successful teams.

Though both Sam and Ken allocate time looking for business, in general Ken focuses more on business development and prospecting and Sam focuses more on deal transactions and client retention. Whitney supports the team in data tracking, analysis, transactional needs and other administrative duties to keep deals moving forward. William will have a role mainly centered on creating new relationships and exposing the team to new opportunities.

The balance of responsibilities can shift based on client needs or preferences. That's easy in a true 50/50 partnership where "we never have to negotiate against ourselves." Since Sam and Ken partner with other teams in their office and around the country, the reality is that every deal is a little different, even though they all follow a similar process.

Everyone is usually involved in deciding on the best way to win a particular piece of business. That includes their firm's marketing staff.

Ideally, Sam will be responsible for fulfilling the business so that Ken is free to go find more business. The men try to have both of them involved during the winning business phase so that a handoff to Sam is easy, but client preferences rule.

Sam draws on support from many sources. Whitney is always at the center of things, but there may also be another junior person or another partner in their office or elsewhere. The team is also keen on using services that their firm provides. Two resources that get a lot of use are the financial modeling team and a project management team that can help keep a project on track through the design, construction and relocation stages.

The team keeps things on track the same way that many other teams profiled in this book do it. They have a regular coordination meeting. Their meeting is every Monday at 8:45 a.m. and lasts about an hour.

They start off the agenda talking about prospecting updates from the previous week. Without sales, no one succeeds. Next, they review any leads that the team has and any critical information about the current pipeline. The rest of the agenda is flexible, depending on what's going on that week. Even though they can see each other's calendars, they've found that it's helpful to take some time to synchronize schedules.

There's an important lesson here about technology. The team makes use of technology, but as a way to help them be more successful. That's true for most teams that use technology well. The magic isn't the technology itself; it's how you use it.

You can have a sophisticated CRM (customer relationship management) system, but it won't do you any good unless you enter your activity into it and use to guide your work. A technology-based calendar allows team members to see each other's schedules, but you get more value from that feature if you also take time to review what team members are doing so you can synchronize your efforts.

Social media is the latest technology craze. But you won't get much value from it if you simply bolt it onto your existing business. The Ashley-Hollis team has based its strategy on building and maintaining long-term relationships, and they've worked out some effective ways to use social media to do that better. They've shaped their use of social media to fit their culture.

SOCIAL MEDIA

Think back to the advice that Mark Christopher gave to Ken. If you want to be successful in commercial real estate, you have to "know your craft." More than that, you have to make people in the marketplace aware of that fact and of what makes you distinctive. You have to tell your story to build market presence. Also, you have to be present and credible in the minds of decision makers when they are ready to look for an advisor on an upcoming real estate transaction. Advertisers spend millions on Super Bowl adds for the same reason: to be on the forefront of someone's thinking when they are ready to make a purchase decision.

Mark's other piece of advice was to think of commercial real estate as a business of "friends and relationships." Building friendships is a long-term process. And friends who are clients are different from people who are only clients. You treat friends differently.

Sam and Ken have worked out a way to use social media to demonstrate their expertise and their low-pressure style so they can build both market awareness and relationships. They use a combination of blogs, LinkedIn and Twitter to make sure that "we're out there and virtually in front of people almost every day." Interestingly, much of this approach revolves around giving away advice, knowledge and information on trends for all to see. In this new world, information, which was formally proprietary (mainly from competitors), is now freely given away in so-called content marketing. "This allows you to showcase your expertise and in doing so build trust and credibility," says Ken.

That takes work, and Ken and Sam share the writing duties. Ken also has developed a system for making sure that he consistently publishes only things (a) that clients or potential clients are likely to find interesting, (b) that help build the Ashley-Hollis brand, and (c) where he "sounds like an adult," meaning he will only talk about professional sounding issues in social media. He calls the system his "Four Corners."

The "corners" are topics that might be interesting to people who read the blog or tweets. Here they are:

1. *Commercial real estate issues.* These include news and trends from the world of commercial real estate.
2. *Management science.* This is Ken's term for an article or post that will help someone do business more effectively. He'll write about topics such as how to be a better leader or build a better team using sources like the Harvard Business Review, CFO Magazine or Forbes.
3. *Technology.* Ken says that "many people find technology

interesting." So he writes about the latest gadget or app and how you can use it to do business better.

4. *Anything positive*. That's what Ken calls the fourth corner. A blog post or tweet about the economic recovery would fit here.

What's just as important is that Ken won't write about anything outside the four corners. There are a lot of other things he could write about, like sports, politics, travel or book reviews. Posts on those topics might be interesting and enjoyable to read. But they don't pass the test of being interesting and helpful for clients and building the team brand. Discipline and consistency in the message is critical.

———————•———————

For a copy of team Ken Ashley's *Social Media Action Plan*, please visit **www.massimo-group.com/TeamBook**. You will need the password "Ashley" (with a capital A) to access this content.

———————•———————

This is a social media strategy that takes commitment. By choosing an aggressive posting schedule and rigorously limiting or focusing the topics, the team produces posts that set them apart from their competition. And it really works, they report. Ken says, "Beyond just Googling you to know you have a real estate license, executives want to hire what they perceive to be the best broker out there."

"We are in many ways a 'blind' purchase, in that it's very hard to tell who is good and who is not. A strong and innovative online presence is comforting to decision makers who think 'where there's smoke there's fire; these guys must be good, given their digital footprint!'"

They differentiate themselves further with the use of another kind of "social" media: in-person special events. As an example, one of the team's marquis events is called "Guns and Grits."

BUILDING RELATIONSHIPS WITH SPECIAL EVENTS

Building a business on relationships means keeping clients at the center and building relationships with them. It also means building relationships with anyone who can help you build your business. The team is also proud of their Southern heritage and sought a way to bring people together to really experience the South.

So, build relationships, expose people to the Southern culture and have fun: Eureka—"Guns and Grits"!

Ken and Sam, along with select sponsor partners, hosts the three-day event at beautiful Burge, which is a private club in the same family since 1809. Important clients are invited, along with Cushman & Wakefield people from all over the country.

The event includes helicopter tours of Atlanta, quail hunts, and the use of a sporting clays course. It's designed to highlight the best of Southern culture and the Ashley-Hollis way of doing business. The events, cocktail hours, and excellent meals (including grits) give everyone the opportunity to intermingle and get to know each other. Here's how Ken describes what happens next:

> We find that the power of a having a couple of dinners together and spending some time talking about our heritage and our culture is that people really have a good time and there's a lot interaction between us and our clients. Leaving our event with great memories, new friends and a smile on your face is just what our Southern mothers would want. From then on, when someone asks you about commercial real estate in Atlanta, we know we will be top of mind.

"But the real magic is they start to interact with each other," says Ken. "That's just great to watch. It's a beautiful thing to see these new relationships and friendships form... and I guarantee you that people will call each other for help on a deal or transaction or perhaps their next job move, based on relationships that were made at our event. Momma would be proud."

In another extension of the event marketing approach, the team also hosts two dinners every year at Sam's home. The first and most important of the two is for the clients they've done business with during the year and their spouses. It's an opportunity to say "thank you" and to demonstrate that Sam and Ken think their clients are special. They celebrate their client's success first and foremost. They find it rewarding to see their clients mingle, share stories and realize that we work hard for a variety of executives in very different industries. They have even seen clients end up doing business together based on these events.

The next night Ken and Sam host a similar dinner for the landlords they've transacted a lease with during the year, along with their spouses. It may seem unusual that a tenant representation focused team would host a dinner party for property owners, but in fact it is a key differentiator for the team's tenant representation clients. Here is how Ken explains it:

> We are in a relationship business, and not just with our clients. Landlords have the power, working through us, to ultimately benefit our clients by making decisions that can have a far-reaching impact. For example, will they grant us an expansion or contraction right that may not be "market?" Will the third-party broker really push an asset manager for another month of free rent or a little more off the rate? These decisions can and do literally result in million-dollar improvements to transactions.
>
> We will do business with many of the same people year after year, and the "favor economy" has helped our clients time and time again, particularly when the market is tight and they need something specific or unusual from their landlord. Put another way, you get a lot more with sugar than with vinegar, especially in a major Southern enclave like Atlanta.
>
> So, about 5 years ago, we started hosting a dinner at Sam's house for landlords with whom we'd concluded a transaction in the previous year. This may seem counter-intuitive because it is the landlords who are typically trying to sell to tenant reps and their clients. However, we certainly realized that landlords or their agents were an important part of the transaction. Clearly, having a good relationship with them could be beneficial in the long run for our clients.

A funny thing happened: The landlords happily attended and were very appreciative at being included. They enjoyed seeing their erstwhile competition at the dinner, and they really had a good time!

Just for fun, the first year we put a bowl near the front door with a sign that said "drop your business card here." After dinner, we held a drawing and gave away some nice bottles of wine and other trinket-type prizes. But one of the most sought-after prizes is one of two Golden Tickets we give away every year.

You see, in order to come to the dinner, you have to have completed a transaction the prior year with our team.

The Golden Ticket winner can come back to the dinner without having completed a deal the following year. Consistently, the Golden Ticket winner has a big smile on his or her face, I think in part because they won something—anything—in front of their competitors.

Our team's landlord dinner is fun ritual that seems to have really caught on with owners and third-party leasing agents alike. The moral to the story is that you can be good to people on the "other side" of a transaction, and have a little fun along the way.

Every landlord in attendance and throughout the market knows we will fight tooth and nail to get the best deal for our clients. However, we believe we are more likely to get a break, when needed, because we treat people on all sides of the transaction with respect, courtesy and a little fun.

These special events are a good example of the Ashley-Hollis relationship-building strategy. They are distinctive, they reinforce the team's brand and they build relationships.

IT'S NOT AS EASY AS IT LOOKS

For the Ashley-Hollis team, everything starts and ends with relationships. Sam and Ken have worked together for almost two decades. They chose to build their business based on the relationships with their clients. That sounds like a good idea to a lot of brokers, but it's not as easy as it might look.

I've witnessed many teams who decide they want to "build their business on relationships." Often that's code for "We don't like to prospect." Often they do the relationship part really well, but they don't have much business success. That's because "building a business on relationships" is harder than it looks.

Building a business on relationships starts with the relationship between Sam and Ken. They took time to develop that relationship. First they worked together, and then they became formal partners. After that, they took some time to "true up" the relationship.

Trust is important. In the early days of their partnership, Sam was the one taking the big risk because he was the one with the book of business. Now that everything is shared equally, they each have trust that the other will put the team ahead of personal ambition. They each assume and, in fact, bet their careers that the other partner is using his time and skills wisely to benefit the team and its clients.

Building a business on relationships means you have to take the long-term view. Relationships take time to develop. You have to give them time to grow and mature. Effective marketing is vital because you have to be top of mind for customers, even when you may not be working with them on a project.

Building a business on relationships means that you have to be clear about which relationships you're going to build your business on. Ashley jokes that they have a "DOGBA—or definition of good business in Atlanta and nationally. For the team, this frequently results in relationships with those midcap companies mentioned early with revenues between $200 million and $2 billion. It can also mean strong and growing local Atlanta companies. "Having airline status is great," says Ashley, "but there is absolutely nothing wrong with working on Atlanta business; it's nice to be home for dinner!" Ideally, the clients are also "brand aware companies" who believe that real estate will help define who they are to clients, customers and other stakeholders. This vision is often a moving target, so you have to adjust constantly.

Building a business on relationships means a different kind of selling. During our interview, Sam described it this way:

> I think it's driven by integrity and a desire to help a client when they need help. We are sales people. That's what we do. I like the way Ken puts it, long term, low pressure.

What's not so obvious is the amount of discipline it takes to build a business this way. It takes discipline to choose potential clients based on whether they fit the profile and then do all the little things it takes to stay top of mind with them. It takes discipline to make sure that every contact moves the relationship forward, even if it's just a little. There's another kind of discipline that Sam and Ken have demonstrated.

In today's business world, there's a lot of pressure to grow by adding more and more people and doing more and more things. Sam and Ken have resisted that pressure. They have kept the team effective by developing junior brokers, while knowing that those brokers would leave and "spread their wings." By adding Whitney and William, they've chosen to grow their team in a way that leverages everyone's talents, and they plan to keep that team intact for a long time.

From the outside, it can look like the Ashley-Hollis strategy is easy or maybe just luck. After all, Sam and Ken don't seem to be chasing new deals with the same intensity as many other successful brokers. Don't be fooled. "Long term, low pressure" works for the Ashley-Hollis team because they have a clear strategy, they organize their efforts based on their strengths and they pay attention to the details. Word of successful execution and a focus on the success of their client's spreads—and Momma would be proud.

IN THEIR OWN WORDS

Sam Hollis

> You have to start with others who complement yourself on the team, because if that fit is not right complementary-skills

wise and personality wise, it will never work. Then you have to operate with mutual respect. There may be a hierarchy on the team, but it can't be a hierarchy that gets in the way of getting the job done. While there is hierarchy, at times everybody has to do something that is a greater task or a smaller task. If you're really working as a team, what you're really trying to do is work toward the same goal. You're not worried about whether you're "above" or "below" getting that task done.

Ken Ashley

In order to work together as a team, you have to have a shared vision, a shared philosophy in life about the way you treat each other and the way you treat your clients. And you have to have offsetting skills. If all partners are good at the same thing, then they probably don't need to work together. If there's a deficit from one person that the other can fulfill, that's the beauty of the team.

And by the way, the team is also a great enabler of lifestyle. If I didn't have Sam, I don't know that I could ever go on vacation. But because I have Sam, Whitney and William, it seems that life's a vacation. At the end of my career, I expect that the dollars will take care of themselves, but the opportunity to have deep and meaningful relationships with team members past, present and future is what I get excited about.

I also take great pride in the 'attaboy' from a client. We do anything legal, moral or ethical to help them succeed— anything. Our mission is not only a great deal, but the perfect fit for their needs. We strive to help the client solve strategic problems with the correct real estate solution. As a team, we try very hard to execute with precision and far exceed expectations of our clients. We are constantly trying to innovate the delivery of our services.

At the end of a transaction, when the executive shakes your hand with a big smile and says, "That was a tremendous deal, and we couldn't have done it without you," that gives me a really deep satisfaction. Like Mark Twain famously said, "I can live for 2 months on a good compliment."

So after 20 years in this business, I've develop a few laws of success:

1. Always be honest.
2. Hard work is not old fashioned. Outwork the competition!
3. Deliver what you say you can, and if possible before you said you would.
4. The client's interests come first. If you center your thinking only about your client's needs, then ultimately you will be that much more successful yourself.
5. Manage client expectations; you should actively work to create the definition of success and get client buy-in.
6. Understand your value proposition and be able to clearly articulate that message to anybody who asks. Why should they hire you?
7. Manage your real estate project team; don't let it manage you. Run the assignment the way you think it should be run. I tell people, this may be your company (or division), but it's my deal to run.
8. Stay in touch regularly; call your client before they call you. The client is counting on your sense of urgency to drive deals to conclusion.
9. Sell and develop relationships to multiple levels within the client company; don't rest on your laurels. I assure you your competitors are not.
10. Focus on the details of a transaction, but be sure and think long term about the client's strategic issues too. They are doing this deal for a reason.
11. Develop personal relationships with clients outside the workday. Those relationships will carry you through the ups and downs and on to new companies with new opportunities!
12. Be an expert in your craft and your market; they expect you to know your stuff.
13. Think, plan, execute; be intentional about controlling

your day. Know what "good busy" is and strive to achieve a high-performance workday every day.

14. Create and develop mentors who will guide you and hold you accountable at every stage of your career.

15. Your success blesses others around you on many levels. Your team, your family and many others in your life are counting on you!

After all of the above, people may not remember exactly what you did or what you said, but they will always remember how you made them feel!

The selfish plus: Remember that you must survive off the fruits of your labor; get commission agreements and letters of representation up front. You are investing your time and expertise in a client; expect loyalty in return or they are not really your client.

The Ashley-Hollis team's story is another excellent example of how teams evolve. First, Ken and Sam were "informal partners." It took several months for them formalize the relationship and then another few years to "true it up" to their current even split. The big shift came when they hired Whitney to be what they call a "client services coordinator." Up until then, they were a pretty standard team with two principals and a rotating cast of junior brokers. Whitney was hired with the intent of upgrading support services so that clients would get better service and Sam, Ken, and anyone else they hire could do more of what they do well.

NEXT UP

The next team in the book has taken the entire concept of high quality support staff one step further. They formed a team to dominate their market and went looking for top notch support staff.

WOSNACK-HARTUM

Team of Specialists

Team Size: 9
Market: Edmonton, Alberta
Focus: Office Leasing; Landlord Representation,
      Tenant Representation

Writer William Gibson likes to say, "The future is already here, it's just unevenly distributed." This chapter about the Wosnack-Hartum team will give you a look at some aspects of the future that are already here when it comes to commercial real estate teams.

So far in this book, I've introduced you to some of today's integrated real estate teams. One thing they have in common is that the support staff are more specialized and knowledgeable than was common just a few years ago. The Wosnack-Hartum team, from Edmonton, Alberta, takes that basic concept one step further. They may give you some ideas of where that trend and others are going.

The team story begins like many other stories in this book. Cory Wosnack and Mark Hartum met when they took the real estate licensing program together in 1995. Cory joined Avison Young, where he started out in office leasing and became one of the dominant agents. He's been a frequent member of Avison Young's Circle of Excellence that honors the firm's top performers.

Mark joined another firm, where his specialty was tenant representation and where he became one of his firm's top producers on national accounts. He and Cory remained friends, even as their firms competed for market share, and they often found themselves on opposite sides of the negotiating table.

Cory and Mark attended each other's weddings. Their personal friendship developed into a close relationship between their families. Somewhere along the way, they must have started talking about working together. Besides being good friends, they also had complementary expertise. So when Cory started thinking about creating a team that would dominate the Edmonton market, he knew that Mark would be an ideal choice.

The problem was that Mark had worked for a decade to build national account business that was contractually tied to the firm where he was. If he left and joined Cory, he would be walking away from 95% of his business. Ultimately, he decided to make the move for three reasons.

First was the opportunity to work with a good friend, someone he could trust, both professionally and personally. Then was the possibility of creating a team that would dominate the market. And finally, was the chance to be part of the kind of team who worked together toward common goals and gave better service to clients. Mark saw it as an opportunity to be part of a different kind of team:

> The previous firm I was at didn't really operate with teams. It was typically an individual broker just working on his or her own files and competing against the other individuals in the office, as well as the competitors across the street. It wasn't really an ideal situation to give the best service to our clients.

By 2005, Cory had hired Peter Schwann, who was just starting to gain momentum in his brokerage career. Mark was working with Karnie Vertz. When they formed the team, Mark and Karnie joined Cory and Peter at Avison Young. For a couple of years they were a "team" in the more traditional sense of the word in commercial real estate. Then, around 2007, they decided to make a major change.

THE BIG SWITCH

Cory says that it's been normal in the business to hire support people who were "pretty good at a bunch of things, but not particularly good at any one thing." That makes sense if you look at costs alone; hiring pretty good generalists costs less than hiring people with developed expertise. The Wosnack-Hartum team decided they wanted to change that.

They wanted to become an integrated team of specialists who would create a strong competitive advantage because the team would do a better job of serving their clients. They believe they can maximize the volume of deals they do and do more of the most influential deals in the marketplace, if they hire only highly capable people for support roles.

The principle is simple. Hire people who have expertise in what you need and who are passionate about the work. Cory uses research as an example:

> You're only as good as the information you have in your toolbox. So we hired someone who loves statistics. Whereas other people can be bored to death with research, we have someone who craves it. Every single day, he's helping us improve our research capabilities.

Today, the team consists of nine full-time people: four principals, two associates, a sales assistant, a client services coordinator and an administrative coordinator. These team members are also supported by a shared research manager, graphic designer and marketing coordinator.

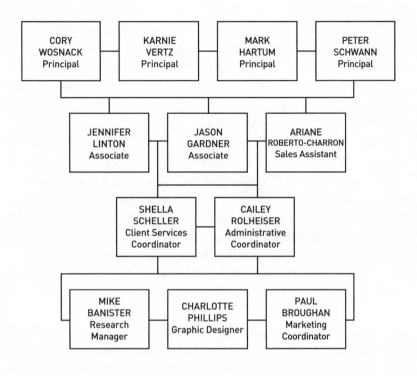

Wosnack–Hartum team organizational chart

Cory says they've really "amped up" their game since they decided to pay a little more and hire people with greater expertise. Of course that means that the team has taken on the challenge of finding and keeping those expert people.

FINDING AND KEEPING EXPERT PEOPLE

Once you decide that hiring the best people for your team is important, the challenge becomes finding and keeping those people. Expertise and passion for the work are not enough. The Wosnack-Hartum Team wants to hire people who have those qualifications, who have a passion for customer service and who fit their team culture, but who aren't exactly the same as the current team members.

They challenge themselves to hire people who will enrich the team and make it more effective, even if that means there are uncomfortable moments because of a clash of personalities or perspectives. That makes hiring even more demanding.

If you follow the principle of expertise, you want to have someone who's good at recruiting run the hiring process. The team could develop that expertise, but that wouldn't be a good use of their time, so they outsource the task to a professional recruiter.

They have been working with the same recruiter for the last 5 years. She's an expert in finding potential hires and screening the ones most likely to work. She can do that because she's taken the time to learn what the team is looking for and the personalities who will fit the culture. When the recruiter has found someone who may fill a need on the team, they begin their own hiring process.

Peter and Karnie do the first interview. If they feel comfortable with the person, Mark and Cory will do separate interviews and then a joint interview. Cory says that they want to be sure that everyone who will work with the person will have a say.

So, does the entire team interview a candidate? Here's Cory's response:

> Yes. However, the final interview is done by the non-principals as a way to test the personality fit. The feeling of inclusion for all existing members of the team ties us together, as we treat the hiring of a new recruit as a group investment. We all need to be invested in the time it will take to get the most of the new member of the team as effectively as possible. We have learned from the past that hiring someone new without the buy-in from the rest of the team, no matter what their role is, will not produce the dividends we strive for. Communication and a feeling of inclusion are key when hiring.

They want everyone on the team to do everything possible to meet their clients' needs and contribute to team success, so there is another step for people in support roles like client services coordinator. The client services coordinator needs to be able to go on tours, speak up about financial issues and be involved in negotiations. That's only possible if the person is licensed, so the licensing program is completed as soon as possible.

Once they're on board, every team member is evaluated every 6 months using a formal process. The core of the process is a five-page list of questions about performance (the past) and development (the future).

———————•———————

For a copy of team *Wosnack-Hartum's Team Member Evaluation* document, please **visit www.massimo-group.com/TeamBook**. You will need the password "Wosnack" (with a capital W) to access this document.

———————•———————

Team members fill out their own evaluation form, and the person most closely aligned with them fills it out as well. This is where it becomes obvious that hiring first-rate people creates a special problem.

The team wants to hire first-rate people and keep them on board for a long time. Keeping them can be a problem because top people are always looking for new and interesting challenges. They can get restless and their performance may decline unless you help them find that new set of challenges. Sometimes the only way to do that is to help them move on.

That's what happened with the woman who was Cory's "right hand" 10 years ago. She now works in another part of the firm, meeting challenges the Wosnack-Hartum team couldn't provide. That's not the ideal, though. Ideally, you want help people expand their horizons without leaving the team.

When I was writing this book, that's exactly what was happening with Jennifer. Here's how Cory describes the situation:

> Jennifer was playing a role of a traditional support individual for years and now she's asked if we can challenge her to be more responsible for bringing in revenue and taking on opportunities to be more like a traditional broker.

We're happy to help fulfill that challenge for her. We don't want her to be confined in a support role when she wants to grow beyond it. So we moved her into an associate role. Now she's bringing in a couple of listings that she will lead. She's going to be more responsible for cold calling and bringing in a certain amount of revenue.

Jennifer wants to stick with the firm and stick with the team but take on some new challenges. Helping her do that is how we keep that loyalty strong.

Finding and keeping great people is one part of the challenge of creating a great team. Another challenge is creating a compensation system that yokes individual effort to team goals and keeps the team moving forward.

COMPENSATION

Effective compensation programs in commercial real estate do two complementary things: They free people up to do the right thing for the client without worrying about how what they do will affect their income; and effective compensation programs also incentivize individual team members to work towards team goals. Here's how the compensation system for the Wosnack-Hartum team works.

Every year they sit down and work out the split for the principals for the year ahead. Once that's done, everyone gets their agreed-upon percentage of every deal, no matter what role they play on the deal.

Full-time support staff are on salary with a bonus that's tied to team achievement. Cory describes how it works this way:

When we produce $1 million, they get bonus. And when we do $2 million, and so and so on. When we get to $5 million, everyone gets a big bonus. And we go on a team trip to Mexico. It doesn't matter if one person is having an off year and another person is a superstar.

As Cory says, when you structure compensation this way, "Revenue is revenue." It all goes into the same pot and then gets split in accordance with the compensation plan. On a practical level, that allows team members to concentrate on finding and winning business for the team.

FINDING AND WINNING BUSINESS

Hockey great Wayne Gretzky played for the Edmonton Oilers for a decade. He learned from his father that "A great hockey player plays where the puck is going to be." The Wosnack-Hartum Team follows the same principle when it comes to finding business. They start by paying attention to trends to figure out where the business is going to be. Cory describes how they work:

> We follow trends that could result in future business opportunities very closely, and there were two burgeoning areas of the city of Edmonton that we anticipated would have a big boost of activity on commercial real estate in the forthcoming couple of years.
>
> One area is called Windermere. Another area is called Summerside. They have turned out to be unbelievable opportunities for us to be the first exclusive listing agents to get into those areas, work with developers, and build a boatload of new office space.

Here's another example. Peter Schwann noticed that medical professionals were moving out of high-rise towers and into low-rise suburban offices. Catching the trend early enabled him to become the top expert in Edmonton on leasing office space to medical professionals.

One exercise we do with our Massimo Group clients begins with asking them to list the first ten names their prospect will think of when they think about commercial real estate. You want your name to be on that list, preferably the first one. Getting out in front of a trend, the way Peter did, almost guarantees a top position in the prospective client's mind. It also ties directly to the strategic planning process.

At the beginning of the year, the Wosnack-Hartum team sets a revenue goal and then develops a strategic plan for how they're going to achieve it. They get specific about which landlords and tenants to go after and what "fields of opportunity" to exploit. Each of the principals takes responsibility for a specific area of practice. They identify everything the team will need to do to achieve their goals.

Building market presence is a key part of the way they find and win business, so the team works hard to make sure that influencers in their market recognize and understand their team brand. Speaking engagements at real estate forums and other industry and civic events are an important part of their presence-building strategy, along with traditional public relations activities.

The team does traditional media activities, like issuing news releases and formal announcements about significant transactions. But they build their team brand by talking about their culture and philosophy, too. Their efforts appear to be paying off.

Last year, Cory was the only person quoted in an article in the Edmonton Journal about what the downtown area will look like at the end of decade. That's impressive, but the media coverage of one of the team's most important deals will give you a better idea of what kind of coverage can result from savvy presence building.

The project was impressive. The team was engaged to advise GE Capital Real Estate on a 220,000 square foot redevelopment project now known as First & Jasper in downtown Edmonton. They took the project from zero to 100% occupancy in 12 months, three times faster than GE projected and at higher rental rates. The media coverage was equally impressive.

The project was featured four times on the front page of the business section of the *Edmonton Journal*. The *Journal's* articles were picked up by other print media in Alberta. There were interviews on both the *GlobalNews* and *CBC* networks, and invitations to speak at two real estate conferences.

That kind of coverage helps you be a person or team that prospective clients have "heard of" when you call. Featuring information about your team and team culture, as well as more traditional information about transactions, helps people know what to expect when you meet them for the first time. That sometimes results in a contact "out of the blue" from someone you've never called on, and it will get you a friendlier reception when you're out prospecting.

No matter how an opportunity surfaces, the Wosnack-Hartum team channels it to the person who's best qualified to handle it. Then the whole team works the opportunity based on the best alignment of team member skills, personality and experience, matched with the client's needs and preferences. It's a true team effort.

GETTING THE WORK DONE

All of the principals on the Wosnack-Hartum team have private offices, with support staff clustered in a bullpen just outside the offices. Many of the teams we've described in this book put everyone in a bullpen so they can hear each other's conversations. Private offices are great for concentration, but they make it hard to have the "accidental sharing" that happens when everyone is close together in the same space. The Wosnack-Hartum team has a unique solution to managing this tradeoff.

They call it their "collaboration area," and its right behind the bullpen. There are comfortable chairs and a whiteboard. The idea is for every internal conversation to happen in the collaboration area, where other team members can hear what's being said and see what gets put on the whiteboard. Naturally that's where team meetings happen.

Every 3 weeks on Wednesday from 3 p.m. until the end of the day, the principals hold a team meeting. They go through "everything that each individual is up to." The support staff members (research, graphic design and marketing) attend every other meeting. The meetings are important and productive, but they're often uncomfortable.

Some of the discomfort grows out of the practice of hiring people with a variety of personalities, and part of it is because every team member has to report on what he or she has done since the last meeting and whether they accomplished what they said they would. They challenge and push each other. The team meeting is the primary way that team members hold each other accountable for the way they're helping to achieve team goals. It's also a key mechanism for team members to communicate with each other about what they're doing.

Between meetings, the Wosnack-Hartum team uses technology in a unique way to keep members up to speed on what's going on. Lots of teams have blogs, but this one has an internal blog that the team has had for a few years. I'll let Cory describe it:

> No one other than the members on our team has access to our blog, and everyone is constantly populating it with all kinds of information. There are all kinds of market news and tidbits of information that people are reporting on daily. When there's something new on the blog, it's automatically sent to our smartphones. One of the simplest yet effective ways for us to keep up with each other is through this blog.

Techies and engineers would call the Wosnack-Hartum team's internal blog an "elegant" solution. That's a term of high praise for anything that uses technology in a way that's simple, easy and powerful.

MOVING FORWARD WHILE KEEPING THE BASICS

One of my favorite quotes about the future is Mark Twain's observation that "History does not repeat, but it does rhyme." No matter how "different" the future will be, there will still be things we recognize from the past. I put the Wosnack-Hartum team in the latter part of this book, because they show you an interesting combination of the things brokers have always done to succeed, and things that may be different in a more team-based industry.

Successful brokers have always looked for ways to be more productive. They've added admin support so they could concentrate on finding, winning and fulfilling business. They've added junior brokers and senior brokers to cover the market more effectively. The Wosnack-Hartum team use the same principles of market specialization, but they've decided that the way to be more productive in the 21st century is to put together a team of specialists who help the team succeed and share in team rewards.

They put together a team of people with different skills and personalities who are willing to work hard together to meet their clients' needs and succeed as a team. They arrange their office space with that in mind. They've structured their compensation so that team success is rewarded and nothing limits a team member's ability to play the role their clients need.

Successful brokers have always looked for a technology edge. The Wosnack-Hartum team does that, too. They use iPads and smartphones and presentation software. And they use the same technology as others in new ways, with their own, internal blog.

The Wosnack-Hartum team is doing many of the same things that have always made commercial brokers successful. But they're doing more, too. They're finding new ways to be successful by creating a team of specialists to meet their clients' needs.

IN THEIR OWN WORDS

Cory Wosnack

It's difficult when you're working in an organization like ours where there are strong A-type personalities. If you just hire more of the same, you're not improving to the full capability that you need. We can't just hire the people that we simply feel our personalities jell with.

We have to challenge ourselves to hire people who are different than us. And we have that diversity. We have hired people whose skills are not the same as our own and personalities that are quite different than ours.

If you look at our support members and if you met them each individually, you'd go, "Wow, I'm surprised that they even all work for the same group because they're just so different." But that difference in their personalities, in their behaviors, results in their having very clearly defined, but different, skill sets. That has produced unbelievable results where every single year we're producing more and more revenue and increasing our market share.

Mark Hartum

> I think it really does come down to a culture. And a key ingredient of our team culture is that we care about each other. We also have very high expectations of ourselves and each other.
>
> We're continuously trying to improve. We hold each other accountable. We really do have a commitment to excellence, and that shows through.
>
> Another important piece of the culture is that we work hard. But we also play hard, and that's part of the balance. And everyone on this team buys into that. And they feel excited to be part of it.

For me, there's a lesson about teams in Mark's experience. Remember that when he left his old firm to partner with Cory, Mark walked away from 95% of his business. There had to be some powerful reasons, and there were. He trusts Cory, and teaming gave them an opportunity to work together and use their complementary specialities to dominate the market. Those are reasons, but they're not new. Mark's other reason was the opportunity to work on a team that made a coordinated effort to reach a common goal, a different kind of team from anything he'd been part of before. The teams I've profiled in this book are the kind of teams where people are willing to subordinate some personal goals to work for the team because they can have more business and life success as part of the team.

NEXT UP

In the next chapter, you'll read about the largest team in the book. In fact, it's really a number of sub-teams with a shared culture and a real "family" feel.

SVN-MILLER

"My Family"

Team Size: 32
Markets: Salisbury, Annapolis and Bethesda, Maryland; and
      Seaford, Wilmington, and Lewes, Delaware
Focus: Commercial Real Estate Sales, Leasing, and Asset/
      Property Management

Henry Hanna, CCIM, SIOR has a picture taken years ago that he'll show you if you ask. It shows a very young-looking Brent Miller, CCIM, CPM, along with John McClellan, CCIM, Chris Davis and Chris Peek, CCIM. If you pick up a copy of Brent Miller's organization chart, you'll find all of those same names, including Henry Hanna.

That's extraordinary, but it's only one of the extraordinary things about Brent Miller's team. His team is the largest in this book and is very successful in a tertiary market. They make effective use of cutting-edge technology, and they have some exceptional HR practices. But the most impressive thing about SVN-Miller is that they're a team that feels very much like a family.

We've all heard people tell us that their team is "just like family." Most of the time that's wishful thinking, but Brent Miller's team feels like a family in a lot of important ways. That feeling and the story of Brent's team start when Henry Hanna recruited Brent to the firm he owned, back in the late '80s, in Salisbury, Maryland. Not only did Henry recruit Brent, but he became a trusted and invaluable mentor, according to Brent.

Henry later sold his firm to Long & Foster, a residential real estate firm, the idea being that Henry's team would become Long & Foster's commercial division. They covered a small market, and most of them were generalists.

Henry is pretty sure that Brent wasn't yet 21 at the time, but Henry was impressed with Brent's determination and drive. Like the others, Brent did retail, office and industrial work; and, like many successful real estate practitioners, he also invested in his craft with Henry's advice and guidance.

With a keen eye for investment opportunities, Brent invested in a 12,000 square foot shopping center. Since there was no one managing the property, Brent saw an opportunity to manage it and get a fee for his work. He set a goal of filling up the shopping center and then selling it at a profit within 5 years.

Brent sold the center to a real estate investor who asked Brent to continue managing it. After he agreed, Brent surveyed the market and decided that there was a property management opportunity for anyone who could do a first-rate job, so he created Miller Property Management to fill that need.

During the next few years, Brent found himself running Miller Property Management and working at Long & Foster doing commercial brokerage. It was working, but it was confusing to his clients who would see his name on different signs around town. He decided it was time to go out on his own and start Miller Commercial Real Estate and Property Management, which would encompass Miller Property Management as well as offer commercial brokerage services.

Although Brent had his own company now, he was still welcome to attend the weekly sales meeting at Long & Foster. This is where you start to get a sense of the high trust levels and family-like feeling that Brent and his colleagues had for one another. Henry trusted Brent to attend his Long & Foster sales meetings and not take competitive advantage of the privilege.

For his first office, Brent purchased a 500 square foot, freestanding corner property. The building had been a drive through, so the footprint was long and thin. There was also an old-style cooler with wooden walls that became Brent's office in the back.

The office was about 6' x 6', with a big cooler door. The area was so small that they had to build Brent's desk inside the office. The firm was made up of an executive assistant, Brent and his wife, Amy. Her Master's-level accounting and marketing skills were a perfect for the growing brokerage and property management companies.

The next big move was to a 1,500 square foot office in a downtown building that Brent owned. This wasn't like the first location with a 6 by 6 office behind a metal cooler door; the new space had a reception area and a conference room. It was time to start expanding.

Brent recruited Rick Tilghman, CCIM as a junior advisor. By now Brent had a pretty good book of business and needed some help on the brokerage side. Here's how he describes the original arrangement with Rick:

> We shared the commissions as a team with the idea that he would be in this training period for ultimately 3–5 years. He could promote himself to a fully commissioned advisor at any time during our relationship.

In this chapter you'll find many ways that Brent gives the people on his team the freedom to make their own choices. You'll also note that he sees himself as the person who can help them identify opportunities and do what's needed to seize them.

The next addition was Brad Gillis, CCIM. Brad already had a book of business, so Brent brought him on as an advisor. At this point, Brent's team was up to five people, and it stayed that way for a few years, until Brent started thinking about another opportunity.

There was no national brand presence in the Salisbury market, but Brent was sure it wouldn't stay that way for long. That led to two more thoughts: the firm affiliated with the national brand would dominate the market, and it might as well be his firm. He started doing research and talking to several national firms.

He liked the fit with Sperry Van Ness (SVN). That led to another idea. Why not put the whole team from the old days back together under the banner of Sperry Van Ness–Miller Commercial Real Estate?

I just saw an opportunity to link my firm with Sperry Van Ness and have these guys be a part of it. It would be a win-win situation for everyone on the team because there was nobody out there providing these types of professional tools or resources and systems in the market.

He started talking to Henry Hanna and the others about the opportunity. Brent knew that it wasn't enough for him to tell them about the possibilities, the culture, the tools, and the resources they would get by affiliating with SVN. They would have to see for themselves and then make their own decisions.

He offered to pay all the expenses to fly his prospective team out to Las Vegas for a 2-day SVN conference. Brent felt the trip would expose his friends and prospective team to the SVN platform and people and reinforce the vision he had for everyone to reunite. And he meant everyone, as did Henry.

Henry says that his group agreed that they would only move to the new firm if everyone was for it. When the time came, that's what they did. Five brokers and their support staff all moved over to Brent Miller's firm. Chris Davis, who was part of Henry's original team, had gotten out of the business, but he came back to join Brent's firm.

The new firm wouldn't fit in the old space, so Brent bought and renovated 5,000 square feet of prime office space in downtown Salisbury, not far from the old office. He wanted to create a "highly professional, first class office space for our clients and for our advisors." The new firm began with a shared history and commitment to a fully commercial real estate group. Brent says they grew around the Sperry Van Ness core covenants and their common vision of giving back to the community.

Those I spoke with said they want to foster the development and growth of the community as a whole and help others who are less fortunate. They've committed time and resources for countless projects for non-profit groups, but they also take time out for fun and teambuilding as well. Their goal is to participate in a minimum of one event a quarter, whether it's building goodwill in the community or building up the team in teambuilding events.

Since 2007, the team has grown dramatically. In addition to the main office in Salisbury, Maryland, there are now five satellite offices in Annapolis and Bethesda in Maryland, and Seaford, Wilmington and Lewes in Delaware. Brent explains:

> One of the main reasons for expanding into other markets in Delaware and Maryland was to expand our footprint and SVN brand awareness. Opening satellite offices in these markets enabled our firm to refer business from office to office (advisor to advisor) and help serve our clients' needs in all markets in Maryland and Delaware. This alignment gave them the opportunity to expand their property management business by offering these services to their associates in a multitude of markets in the East Coast.

The internal teams have their specialties. The Hanna Team (consisting of Henry Hanna, Wesley Cox, CCIM and Flo Adams) focuses on industrial, Alder Land Group (consisting of Ben Alder and Nick Campanaro) focuses on land and agriculture and Team Devreco (consisting of Bradley Gillis, CCIM, Joey Gilkerson, Chris Gilkerson and Mike Bireley) focuses on professional/medical office space. McClellan's team (consisting of John McClellan CCIM and Emily Rohrer) and Brent's team focuses on retail. Other individual advisors have their own specialties in areas like multi-family, self-storage and hospitality.

In many ways all the teams are autonomous. Brent encourages that by giving team leaders a lot of freedom to make choices about how they work, about some aspects of compensation and about technology.

BIGGER THAN YOUR AVERAGE TEAM

Brent's "team" is the biggest one I studied. And many people contend that it's far too big to be considered a true team.

When most people think of "teams," they usually conjure up a sports team of some kind. But sports teams have a specified size that every team in the sport conforms to. In the rest of life and in business, we use the word "team" much more loosely.

We have all heard the CEO of some giant industrial corporation refer to his hundreds of thousands of employees as a "team." When most people think about a "team" in business, though, they're thinking of a fairly small group of people who know each other and coordinate their efforts to reach a shared goal.

Teams like that have become common in business. That's driven academic researchers to conduct studies of ideal team size. Evan Wittenberg, director of the Wharton Graduate Leadership Program, summarizes the research by saying that ideal team size "does tend to fall into the five to twelve range, though some say five to nine is best, and the number six has come up a few times."

So, is Brent Miller's team a real team? Brent has done a fantastic job of creating a firm with a number of productive sub-teams. That part isn't unusual. What makes Brent's firm unique is that those sub-teams operate in a very strong culture of cooperation and collaboration and that there are many strong relationships between individual members of different sub-teams.

In fact, the firm and the sub-teams are both real teams. They both are made up of people who know each other and coordinate their efforts to reach a shared goal.

Brent Miller's team is larger than most teams in another way, too. His team consists of a brokerage and also a property management company.

THE PROPERTY MANAGEMENT BUSINESS

The property management company has grown since Brent was doing everything himself. Amy is the Director of Property Management and the CFO of the firm. Brent and Amy see the property management company as a perfect fit with the brokerage.

SVN-Miller is selling and leasing commercial properties, and it just makes sense to market the property management business at the same time. The two companies share marketing staff, which makes it easy for them to coordinate their efforts. Brent says one of their most effective marketing tools is signage:

We have these property management identifiers (small signs) that just say "Property managed by Sperry Van Ness" with the SVN-Miller Commercial Real Estate hologram. This little sign sits in a nice landscape area somewhere highly visible. It's not a big sign, maybe a foot by eighteen inches, not gaudy at all. It's just enough to where the public can see who manages the property.

It must be working because Brent says they've increased the square footage under management in every single year of the business, even during market downturns. Of course, marketing is only part of the secret of success; the more important part is how you deliver service. That's up to the property managers.

The firm currently has two property managers. Rick Tilghman, CCIM started out as a junior broker under Brent and moved over to become a senior advisor concentrating on leasing and also a property manager. The other property manager is Brent's brother, Bart.

Their property management philosophy is to retain tenants and increase the client's net operating income. Brent thinks you make that happen by delivering professional services and developing relationships with tenants. He captures those two objectives in his mantra: "The property management business is a tenant relationship business." That makes sense: retention through attention.

The key activity that drives the quality management and relationship building is a full-blown inspection of every property at least once a month. That responsibility falls to the property managers: Brent's brother, Bart, and Rick Tilghman, CCIM.

Bart and Rick are in the field a majority of the time. Their iPhones and iPads, combined with Yardi software, give them the ability to do anything that a property manager could do in the office and still spend the time on site to handle inspections and relationship building.

The property management company has had to add people constantly as the amount of property under management has risen. And adding people is something Brent does very, very carefully.

The ability to find and win Property Management business is a critical component to many commercial real estate organizations. However, these team leaders generally have personalities different from those of brokerage team leaders. We have successfully worked with scores of property managers across the country and assisted them in getting in position to secure property management assignments immediately and in the long-term as well. For more information regarding our Property Management Coaching, please visit **www.massimo-group.com/coaching**

GROWING THE TEAM

As you might expect with Brent's success and visibility, lots of people want to join the firm. When that happens, he does a lot to increase the odds that anyone he brings on board will be a good fit, both professionally and personally:

> It's like we are a family and we are adopting a child. And we have to do the proper due diligence to bring somebody into our family because one bad apple can ruin a firm.

Many firms have a formal hiring process. Brent has a process, but it isn't formal. Brent's process consists of three kinds of assessment, all of which Brent uses to guide his judgment. It usually begins with talking to the candidate.

In a phone and in-person interview, Brent gets an initial assessment of the candidate. He's seeking information about the candidate's life history and achievements and why he or she wants to join Brent's team. He's also assessing the candidate as a person and as a worker. How does the person come across in person and on the phone?

Throughout the entire process, Brent is working to assess two things. The new person must bring something that will help make the business better. And the candidate must fit with the team. He or she must have the same values and work ethic and a personal style that fits with the other team members.

The due diligence process involves taking the time to test initial impressions. That includes verifying credentials and work history. It may involve checking out the person's social media presence and how they act.

Brent will ask team members about the candidate. This is a situation where it's an advantage to be working in a smaller market, because Brent will probably know a lot of people who know the candidate. He'll talk to everyone he can, gathering impressions. If things still look good, a formal psychological assessment is next.

Brent does a psychological assessment of everyone he might ask to join the team. That includes both advisors and any other employee. He uses the AVA instrument. We will explore this instrument in great detail later in this book.

The AVA instrument does three things. First, it gives Brent a way to either verify or question the assessment he's developed up to this point in the process, especially about whether the candidate will fit into the team. Second, comparing the candidate's profile against the profile of people who perform well in the same role helps Brent evaluate whether the candidate will succeed in the role. The assessment also gives Brent a management and coaching tool he can use after the person is on board.

I've seen too many firms that think the hiring process is done when the new person shows up for work on the first day. But hiring and productivity experts say that onboarding is every bit as important as the hiring process.

Brent makes it mandatory for every new advisor to attend SVN boot camp. He also requires every advisor to either have their CCIM or be working toward it. Brent claims that SVN-Miller has more CCIMs than any other firm in the State of Maryland.

As the team grows, so do the challenges of coordinating the efforts of sub-teams, maintaining the culture of the whole team, and allowing sub-teams the freedom to do things in the way that works best for them. Technology is part of the answer to those challenges.

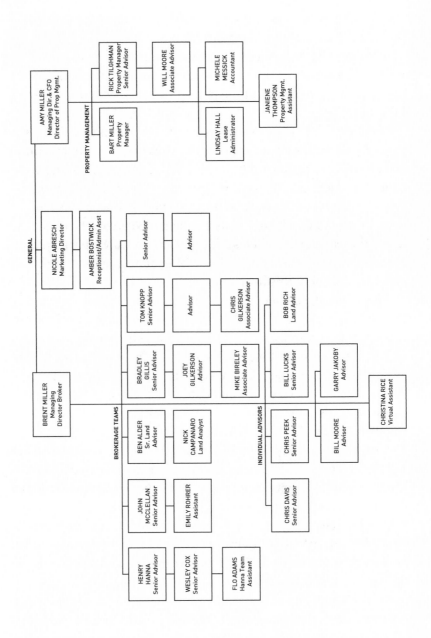

Sperry Van Ness–Miller Commercial Real Estate organizational chart

TECHNOLOGY

It's easy to get caught up in the "whiz-bang" discussions of technology. Too many firms in the marketplace brag about having the latest and greatest technology, but they don't seem to have given much thought to how the technology will help do more and better business. Successful firms, like SVN-Miller, are always thinking about that. Take drones, for example.

Someday drones will be a regular and unremarkable part of the business landscape. But today, SVN-Miller's drone helps give them a competitive advantage. It says to potential clients that this is a savvy and sophisticated company. And it sends the message to insiders that Brent is committed to giving them state-of-the-art tools for doing business.

When I analyze Brent's use of technology, it fits with the way he manages the firm as a whole. The drone is a good example.

Everything he chooses fills a need. There are no "Gee whiz" or "just for show" choices. The drone is distinctive. For now at least, it sets SVN-Miller apart from other firms in the area. Because it's new and progressive, the drone adds a "Wow" factor. It also helps SVN-Miller present properties and win listings more effectively.

Every bit of technology fits into a system. The drone isn't simply bolted on to the way the firm does business. Nicole Abresch, head of the marketing department, takes the images and video and manipulates them to make them better. She cleans up the images and adds music or a voiceover to take the pictures/videos to the next level of professionalism. Then they are stored on the firm's server and on Google Drive so any team members can get them and use them.

The 60-inch flat screen with speakers in the Salisbury office also provides an example of using technology effectively. It's a great venue to bring clients and show the professional quality video. But it's also an important tool to help SVN-Miller coordinate activities and maintain important relationships.

The system has a web cam so that when SVN-Miller has their Tuesday all-hands meeting, everyone can attend. They can all be seen and heard, whether they're in the main office, a satellite office, a home office, or any other location where the technology is available.

SVN-Miller uses technology to make it easy for anyone in the firm to work where and how they think is best. Bart Miller does most of his work from his technology-equipped truck. Christina Rice, Brent's assistant, works mostly virtually. Advisors can be in the office, at home, in a client's office, or anywhere else.

Using Google Drive and Google Apps makes it easy to store, sync and share files, no matter where you are and no matter what technology you happen to be using. When an advisor is negotiating a lease, for example, everyone involved can work with a single document. If someone buys a new phone or tablet, they can update their contact list in seconds from data stored in the cloud.

Brent also gives his sub-teams a lot of latitude about what technology they want to use. CRM (database) software is a good example.

In many firms the choice of what CRM software to use is made at the top, and everyone uses the same system. Brent has taken a different approach. Everyone uses a CRM system, but internal team leaders make the call on what system to use.

Henry Hanna's team had been happy with the CRM software they'd used for years. But they kept hearing from others about how this program or that would serve their needs more effectively. So, for a couple of years, they tried other systems. In the end, though, they went back to what they had used before.

Brent's view is that people are more likely to use a software program they like, so if the program does the job it's fine. In this case, Henry's team didn't want to waste time learning another program that didn't have a significant added value for them.

KEEPING THINGS ON TRACK

A team leader really has two jobs, according to many leadership gurus. One job, the one we talk about most, is to help the team as a whole succeed. The other job is to help individual team members succeed. Many leaders say they do both. Brent Miller really does.

Some of the things Brent does are common to other people who lead an effective team. He insists that everyone have goals, a business plan to achieve them and a way to track them. He meets with his advisors regularly, every month in his case, to review progress. But for Brent, that's where things get much more personal:

> Their goals are their goals. I don't tell them what their goal should be. I don't tell them what's important to them. They create their own goals. And I help them and guide them on achieving those goals.

The goals they talk about are more than business goals, if that's what an advisor wants. Brent thinks that a well-balanced life will help anyone be more successful in commercial real estate. So he encourages the team to include other goals and aspirations in their discussions. He understands his role as helping the others sharpen their goals and develop a plan to achieve them, and then make that plan work.

He helps them figure out what they need to do this year, next year, and several years out. Then they work out what the other person needs to do daily and weekly and monthly now, to make those goals happen. Every set of goals is unique because every associate is unique.

That means each person will have slightly different metrics. One might track listings and another might track phone calls. When it's time to meet, Amy provides a spreadsheet that tracks their gross commission income (GCI) and other goals for the year to date. Brent then builds his performance review around the data. He and Amy do the same thing when they review performance for the firm.

They have a budget for everything. There are metrics for the individual offices and for property management and for the firm as a whole. Once a month, Brent and Amy sit down and go over all of it. It's the hard-numbers side of their management style.

One thing that makes SVN-Miller successful is a hard-nosed approach to business. But there is also a strong emphasis on people and relationships. That helps make them successful, but it also makes them unique.

MY FAMILY

When we were talking about hiring and growing the team, I asked Brent about the reasons he has let people go. "I don't think I ever let anybody go," he replied.

I couldn't believe it. That's amazing. Brent hires well and manages the onboarding effectively. There's a probationary period where Brent monitors the new person closely, so problems are caught early and changes get made quickly. That's effective, but new people are willing to change because they want to stay at SVN-Miller.

Brent and Amy make sure that SVN-Miller is a great place to work. It's like a family. Really. Lots of people claim that for their team, but this team feels like one. Brent says that's the "juice" in this team. The engagement that you see at SVN-Miller grows out of a number of what seem like "little" things. Many of those things are just people doing things together.

People come together for meetings and people who work virtually spend time in the office. And there are the team-building activities similar to what many other teams do. When people spend a lot of time together, they build close relationships.

The team is embedded in the community. There's time at the all-hands meeting to talk about community news and the team's community projects. The projects include work at Habitat for Humanity and an annual river clean-up.

Those are the sorts of things that might seem all warm and fuzzy, but they're coupled with things that build business efficiency. Brent and Amy make sure that people at SVN-Miller have the equipment and resources they need to do good work. They're committed to helping people achieve their goals and willing to adapt to changing life circumstances.

That relationship building pays off every day, but it can be especially important when things get tough. In October 2012, Super Storm Sandy roared up the East Coast. Salisbury was one of the cities in its path. The mayor declared a state of civil emergency as streets and buildings were buffeted by the winds and flooded by the water.

When he was able to, Brent went to the office in Salisbury. As he walked through the office, he shot video of damaged walls and furniture and floating wastebaskets. They put a plan in place to have the office functional again by Thanksgiving, just a few weeks away. They got it done.

The entire team, including some spouses and children, pitched in to move things out, rebuild and redecorate the office, and move back in before Thanksgiving. It was the kind of success you want to celebrate, and part of the celebration was ringing their success bells.

Different teams have different ways to celebrate success. SVN-Miller has their success bells.

After Brent had sold a building to the State of Maryland, he discovered that the previous owner had left a set of bells there. They had used the bells to let staff know when someone came in through the door. The State didn't want them because they would have a state-of-the-art security system. The previous owner didn't want them anymore, either. So Brent adopted them. I'll let him describe how they're used now:

> The bells hang on a plank right in the middle of the hallway in the office. Anyone that has any type of success can go by and ring those success bells. Maybe you're excited about getting your listing, you just did a big sale, you just had a settlement, you just found out you are pregnant, anything. People just go by and they ring the bells.
>
> And what happens is people come out of the woodwork. Obviously if you ring the success bell you want to tell other people about your success and you want them to join in your celebration.

We all celebrate together. And it's just that camaraderie and networking together that really sets us apart and makes us a good family company.

IN THEIR OWN WORDS

Brent Miller

I always say to my team that what you focus on is what you will achieve. And focus starts with setting good goals. I think good goals are SMART goals, meaning, Specific, Measurable, Attainable, Realistic and Timely.

If you have written goals, then you focus on these goals. You review them on a regular basis. And you keep working towards achieving them.

You might have a large goal and smaller goals that you need to accomplish so you achieve that large goal. What you focus on you will achieve. And that's life. That is not business, that is life.

Henry Hanna

I think it's very important to be careful about who you invite into the team. We've had people who had approached us in terms of SVN-Miller. I think Brent almost always, at some point in that process, talks to everybody else within the office to say, "This is who I am talking to. Do you have any comments or thoughts about it?"

Especially now that we are kind of growing outside of the small geographical area of Salisbury, he solicits thoughts before a decision is made. I think we have avoided some problems by not taking some people into the team because we didn't think they would fit or they didn't bring in the same values.

John McClellan

You have to ask yourself: Are you the kind of person who wants to have a team and if you are a good coach and you can really develop somebody, or whether you are the kind of person who's looking for somebody to take some of your load on?

If you are the person who can develop, coach and take a man or woman who is relatively new to the business and really coach them and take ownership of them and build them up, then you are the kind of person who should probably look for a junior. If you are the kind of person who just needs somebody to help you carry your load, then you want to look for more of an administrative person, a marketing person, a social medial person, somebody who has those kinds of skills.

SVN-Miller is a prime example of handling the twin challenges of teams that dominate. The scientific research on teams mentions that successful teams have two components. One is business. Teams that dominate have processes and systems and policies that make sure the business gets done. Teams that dominate also do things to create a common culture and support team members. SVN-Miller does both of these well, even with the largest group in this book.

NEXT UP

The final team profile in this book is the Coppola-Cheney team. Craig Coppola gave me the phrase "integrated team," that I've been using because it's an excellent description of teams built to dominate. As you read the chapter on the Coppola-Cheney team, pay special attention to all the things they've done to align efforts and interest so the team really is making a coordinated effort toward a common goal.

COPPOLA-CHENEY

The Integrated Team

Team Size: 7
Markets: Phoenix, Arizona
Focus: Commercial Real Estate Tenant Representation

You can divide Craig Coppola's commercial brokerage life into two successful parts. There is the part where he became a top producing salesman, and then there is the integrated team where the team became the top producing office team of all time at Lee & Associates.

Craig started in the business in 1984. In 1991, he was one of the founding principals of Lee & Associates, Arizona. At the time, the office was the tenth office for the firm and the first one outside of California. The Phoenix office has been the top producing Lee & Associates office for 20 of the past 23 years.

In the beginning, Craig's team was what many brokers call a team today. There was Craig, a runner, and an admin assistant. For a little more than a decade, that's how things stood.

Every 2½ years or so, he would take on a new runner. Craig thinks of a runnership as "an audition for partner," and he's an enthusiastic and effective trainer and coach who loves "working with young people to make a career for them." He has his 2½-year development program laid out, and he's constantly improved it over the years. Today, he is training his ninth runner.

For a copy of team *Coppola-Cheney's Runner Job Description*,
please visit **www.massimo-group.com/TeamBook**.
You will need the password "Coppola" (with a capital C)
to access this document.

Craig believes that a person learns the business by doing it over and over and over. That's in line with one of the dominant theories of development, that people get only about 10% of their learning from books and formal classes. The vast majority, 90%, comes from working on the job and from coaches, mentors and peers. This is the primary reason we coach at the Massimo Group and simply do not *train*.

The first year is devoted to what Craig calls "back stage" work that exposes the runner to the business and the workflow associated with the business. Back stage includes things like putting together tour packages and doing research; learning the systems, programs and pace of a transaction. There are no client presentations, but there is plenty of detail work. During the second year, the new broker starts working on small transactions "that we can afford to let him learn the job on." Moving into the third year, the broker will be doing more and larger transactions.

Craig has trained eight runners—four still working at Lee & Associates Arizona. Andrew Cheney was the first one Craig wanted to partner with on his personal team. Craig says that he didn't find Andrew. Andrew found him.

Andrew says that as a boy he "always wanted to be a professional tennis player, then some sort of businessman." Tennis careers start early, especially in a tennis family. When Andrew was a boy, playing in junior tournaments in Arizona, he could get a workout and a few pointers from his grandmother, Dorothy "Dodo" Cheney. Dodo, who died in November 2014, is a member of the International Tennis Hall of Fame.

After finishing college, Andrew spent 4 years on the pro tennis tour before deciding it was time to become "some sort of businessman." He chose commercial real estate because of the "income potential, freedom and the chance to learn about many different businesses."

Once he knew what he wanted to do, the next step was to find a good coach. Andrew says that his tennis experience taught him the importance of having a good coach. Take two players with equal natural talent, and the one with better coaching will become a better player. He wanted to work with someone who was a great coach, so he did his homework.

He asked around and talked to a lot of people. Andrew still had a string of interviews set up when he connected with Craig. They both thought they had a good fit. Andrew cancelled all the interviews he had scheduled and joined Craig's team. Craig thought Andrew might be the perfect fit for the kind of team he wanted to build.

Craig likes hiring people with an athletic background because they understand "dedication, focus and putting in long hours." He also knew that Andrew came from a great family. Putting those two things together, he figured that Andrew would fit into the team and work hard. He knew Andrew brought unique abilities that would enrich the team.

Craig wants to hire people who have different unique abilities than his. He calls himself "a collector of unique abilities." Craig has a degree in finance and an MBA. Andrew's degree is in civil engineering. He would help form the foundation to become the kind of integrated team that Craig had been thinking about for a while.

Craig spends time thinking about how the business is changing and what the future might bring. Those topics are a regular feature in the team newsletter. He saw that the business was becoming more complex and sophisticated. Clients were demanding different services. Craig believed the future would belong to teams, and not just any kind of team. He wanted to build an integrated team of "good people," with a strong work ethic and unique abilities. Andrew was his first hire for that kind of team.

Andrew became a partner in 2006. He's the main point of contact for major listings and tenant representation assignments, and he provides market updates to all the team's clients. Andrew also is responsible for strategic planning and negotiations.

The other partner is Gregg Kafka, who came on board as a runner in 2011 and became a partner in 2013. He has an extensive background in construction management and assists with research and market analysis, touring, broker's opinions of value (BOVs), lease review, acquisition of new clients, tenant rep assignments and managing a portion of existing listings.

In 2011, Chelsea Clifton was hired as an admin assistant. She's now director of operations, responsible for client correspondence, project management, preparation of marketing packages and client presentations, contact database management, and general administrative duties.

Erica Bradley joined the team in 2013 as strategic assistant. She is responsible for general administrative duties, client tour schedules, organizing of calls and schedules, marketing emails and social media. Both Erica and Chelsea have their Arizona Real Estate license. A requirement for the team is a license. In addition to the core, the team consistently has two to four interns at any given time. These are in addition to the staff provided by Lee & Associates to perform such responsibilities as secretarial, graphics, research and mapping.

That's how the core team sets up today. They're the top performing team of all time at Lee & Associates. Craig describes their business as tenant and landlord representation in the office sector, local, regional, and national. About 15% of the business is sales, but only if they're part of the project or have a relationship with the owner. Tenant representation contributes 55% of revenue, and the remaining 30% comes from representing landlords. Their time however, is spent 55% on listings and 25% on tenant representation.

GOD IS IN THE DETAILS

Like many of the teams in this book, the Coppola-Cheney team works close together in an open bullpen space. But there are some key differences from the way other teams work that grow out of some careful thinking about how to be productive.

You won't hear the clicking of computer keys as the partners make notes during a call. Instead team members take all their notes by hand. It's not because they don't have or use the latest CRM, because they do. The reasons relate to the client experience and productivity.

Craig says that he doesn't want any distractions for team members or the client during a call, and that includes the clicking of keys. So team members take their notes by hand and turn them over to a data entry person (an intern), who puts them into the CRM system. Distraction is only one reason, though.

Craig has put the team together and structured operations so people can use their personal unique skills to add value to the process. Data entry is simply not a value-adding skill. That's why it's outsourced, so that team members can spend most of their time doing what they do best to make the team productive.

That's just one example of the little things the Coppola-Cheney team do that reflect Craig's view of the world and the best way to do business. To understand them, you need to know a little about Craig and his background.

Ralph Waldo Emerson said that "an institution is the lengthened shadow of one man." If he were writing about teams, he would probably say the same thing about them, and he could certainly describe the Coppola-Cheney team as the lengthened shadow of Craig Coppola.

Craig believes that no matter what you go for, you should go for it 100%. That's brought him great business success and a lot more. He's won a world championship in Tae Kwan Do and run more than 80 marathons and ultramarathons. He's also authored three books:

> I never wanted to be second best. I don't want it in my business or personal life. I don't want it in my athletic life. I don't want it in my relationship life. I want to be the top.
>
> I was the number one guy at Lee before Andrew joined me. And our team is now the number one team in the office now that Andrew is on board. And I'm not saying it's me, but our team is a reflection of who I am. And who I am is that we're going to win at everything we do.

Craig identifies two kinds of brokers. He calls one kind "processors." When they work on a deal, they don't do much more than passing information and requests back and forth. Craig and Andrew demand something different on their team. They want engaged, trust-building brokers who add value to every transaction, at every stage of the process. And they want the team to excel.

Two of Craig's favorite words are "unique" and "alignment." They come up again and again when you talk to him about how the team works, and they explain why the Coppola-Cheney team does things the way they do. Compensation is a good example.

ALIGNING INTERESTS THROUGH COMPENSATION

Most teams have some kind of origination bonus that gives more to the person who originates a deal. This team doesn't do that. Instead, the three producers get a fixed percentage of the revenue from every deal, and that percentage stays the same for a year.

At the start of every year, the partners negotiate the split for the coming year. That's intended to align their efforts with the interests of their clients and the overall success of the team. The support staff gets a salary plus bonus. The key to it all is a ruthless focus on the numbers.

To make sure that works and that interests are aligned, the Coppola-Cheney team practices open-book management. That term was coined by *Inc.* magazine writer John Case, back in the 1990s. The basic idea is that when people understand the cost structure and how the organization is doing, they're more productive.

GETTING THE WORK DONE

Those same principles of using everyone's unique abilities, working toward the same goal and aligning everyone's efforts also show up in the way that the team handles deals. Here's how Craig describes that process:

> We're an integrated team, so every team member will touch almost every transaction. We can do that because of the way we've aligned our compensation.

What we do is client-specific on all transactions. So if we have a large assignment that is complex and they need my 30 years of experience, I'll be involved in it. If it's a smaller transaction that's fairly straightforward, Gregg will run with it. If it's a medium transaction, Andrew will handle it. He and I will work on all the bigger complex transactions together. Our staff will also work on all the back stage stuff, including tour packages, building calling, those kind of things.

Because of the integration, we look at the client's requirement, and then we kind of decide how we're going to work it.

Every team I researched has regular meetings of some kind to coordinate their effort. The Coppola-Cheney team has meetings, too, but they have a very different cadence from most teams.

Every Friday, there's a quick email update of calls and business. Since the team works together in a tight bullpen, team members usually have a pretty good idea of who's doing what, so the email update is a check on that awareness.

Most teams I researched have a weekly team meeting, but this team meets about ten times a year. The meetings are held on a Saturday. "Why?" you ask. Andrew's answer: "We'll never meet during selling hours."

Every month, the partners have what they call a TIP meeting. TIP stands for Transactions in Progress. Other teams call this a pipeline review. TIP meetings are on Saturday morning and usually take between 2 and 3 hours.

Every team profiled in this book works hard, especially team Coppola. Their work schedules also demonstrate how they combine the principles of "alignment" and "unique." The partners are all aligned on the principle of working hard and putting in the hours. But they each set their own unique schedule, based on their private lives and personal preferences. Here's a quick overview of how that works in a normal week.

Craig rolls out of bed at 3:30 a.m. and is exercising by 4:00 a.m., 6 days a week. He's in the office by 7:30 and works until his day ends and he goes home for dinner. Craig doesn't exercise on Saturday, so he's in the office by 4:00 a.m. and works until around noon.

Andrew is a night person. He gets into the office around 8:00 a.m. every day and works until 5:30 or 6:00. Then he works out and has dinner, after which he heads back to the office for another 2 or 3 hours. On Saturdays he's at the office around 9:00 or 10:00 a.m. and works until 3:00 or 4:00.

Gregg is in the office weekdays by 5:30 a.m. and works until 6:00 p.m. He also works 3 or 4 hours on Saturday.

You may be thinking to yourself that the numbers of hours Craig, Andrew and their team put in are unreasonable. As I shared in my first book, *Brokers Who Dominate*, dominant commercial real estate professionals are entrepreneurial. They have the correct perspective. This isn't a 9–5 job; this is their personal, professional business.

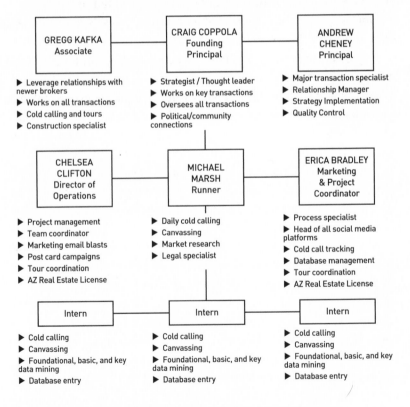

Coppola-Cheney organizational chart

HIRING NEW PEOPLE

Those are long hours by any standard. Not everyone can or will want to work like that, but it's important for the team that everyone on the team has the same values. That's one of the things they'll look for when they bring another person on, but they'll also want unique abilities that add value to the team and a person who understands the focus on achievement.

There's no formal hiring process, but there are two things that happen for every hire. The Coppola-Cheney team uses a psychological assessment to make a judgment about whether a new person will fit the team. Everyone on the team will interview a candidate, too.

Once a new person is on board, you can expect Craig to devote time to helping them grow and develop. He wants people to stay for a long time and, as he says, "If you spend your days doing what you truly love to do, and you make a lot of money, why would you ever leave?" It must be working because the average tenure of brokers at Lee & Associates Arizona is almost 20 years.

There have been a lot of changes in the last 20 years, and there are still more to come. Like other teams in this book, the Coppola-Cheney team is constantly watching trends and figuring out what to adopt right away.

LEADING EDGE, NOT BLEEDING EDGE

The Coppola-Cheney team is a great example of how "sophisticated use of technology" doesn't necessarily mean "technology leader." Like other teams that are savvy users of technology, they choose what they do and don't do, based on their clients and the way they do business.

They have a CRM database but take notes by hand during phone calls. Then someone else enters the notes into the database. But they've also synced their phones to the database, so they can update a client record right from the phone.

They use InDesign and PowerPoint for materials and presentations. They know that other brokers are doing iPad presentations, but they haven't tried that yet. They find that their client meetings are more likely to be discussions than presentations.

They're active in social media, on Facebook, Twitter, and Google+. But they're not depending on social media too much right now because their clients aren't spending very much time there. They're watching the trends, though, and they're sure that will change as more and more as younger people move into responsible positions.

One of their most effective marketing efforts is a mix of the old and the new. It's a weekly email newsletter called *My Narrative* that goes out to a list of about 25,000. It's Craig's narrative about the office market, real estate, or some other story he finds interesting.

One recent issue will give you a sense of how they work. The headline was "7 Bold Commercial Real Estate Predictions." It featured an article by a real estate expert, along with Craig's opinion on the significance of the article. The article itself is highlighted so readers can easily scan it for important relevant information. The narrative also included a picture of Craig and another Lee & Associates partner standing at the top of Mount Kilimanjaro, Africa's highest peak, and showing a Lee & Associates banner. There's also a link to a slide show that Craig created about the expedition.

Email newsletters are not cutting-edge technology. But Craig's narrative is an excellent use of a proven technology. It provides information that will interest people who sign up for the newsletter while branding the Coppola-Cheney team as trend watchers and thought leaders. It also shares something interesting about the team. That's what good marketing communications are supposed to do.

The Coppola-Cheney team is one of the hardest working teams in this book. Like the other teams we've profiled, they do a lot of things right and they do some unique things that may give you some good ideas.

They're also a good example of a team that was consciously designed to be the kind that will succeed in today's commercial real estate environment. They call it an "integrated team." That starts with recognizing the unique ability that every team member brings. As Craig has said, "Everyone has a unique ability, and on our team each person has one that is different from mine."

Those unique abilities are important, but by themselves they only create a group of talented people. The Coppola-Cheney team members are selected based on common values and work ethic.

That's another important piece, but to create a truly effective team you must unite the team members around a common purpose and goal. On this team the numbers rule, and everyone knows the numbers.

Finally, the Coppola-Cheney team has gone to great lengths to make sure that individual and team interests are aligned. That's what brings the unique abilities, the hard work, and the common purpose and goals together and makes for exceptionally impressive performance.

IN THEIR OWN WORDS

Andrew Cheney

I would say that key components of a great team are culture, respect, thoughtfulness and focus. You have to respect each other. That builds trust. Thoughtfulness stems from that. And you need people who are aligned with your focus.

Erica wants to succeed. She wants to get better. Chelsea is constantly growing as well. Gregg wants to be a top producer. Craig, even being the #1 guy, still wants to. I sure as hell want to get better and want to be in Craig's position when I'm his age. And we all have aligned goals and want to improve, and we just respect each other.

Craig Coppola

Well, the number one thing to create a great team is that you have to have great quality people. You have to hire just the best people. And we have made mistakes where we didn't have the quality person who was raised right. But, if you come in and meet our team, you would just go, "Those are really good people."

The second part is that you take great quality people who have different unique abilities and create a team based on their unique abilities. So quality people, unique abilities.

If you take these great people who have different unique abilities, you give them a clarity of purpose—here's what we're trying to do, so we all know what we're trying to do at all times—and you put it into alignment. You align their work habits and their financial rewards and their work hours and how they're treated, you align their clarity of purpose and then you'll have a team that's fabulous.

So quality of people, unique ability, clarity of purpose, and alignment on all the goals.

Now you've had an in-depth look at eleven commercial real estate teams built to dominate. Before you move on, why not take a moment to review your notes and highlights. Then when you're ready, turn the page for my final thoughts—or should I say "almost final?" Remember to read the lesson-packed Team Science chapter.

CONCLUSION

Teams Built to Dominate

When I began researching this book, I was sure of two things. I knew that more and more leading commercial real estate professionals were choosing to work in teams. I was sure that some of those teams were dramatically more effective than others. I wanted to discover the "whys" behind those two things.

So I embarked on a multi-year study of teams, specifically teams in commercial real estate. I asked myself questions like "Why are we seeing top producers shift to a teaming model?" One answer was that there are powerful shifts happening in our business that make teams a better way to do business. I outlined those shifts in detail in the Introduction, but here they are again in brief.

1. There is more complexity than ever before.
2. Fulfillment has become more comprehensive.
3. There are more multi-location client opportunities today than ever before.
4. Access to information is greater than at any time in our lives and will only continue to grow.
5. Leveraging Skills in a team environment is vital.
6. A culture of collaboration is more common.

I needed to learn something about teams in general, what scientists have to say about all kinds of teams. So I read a lot and consulted experts to help understand what I call "The Science of

Teams." You'll find an in-depth review of what I learned in the next chapter.

I also realized that I already had an amazing resource: our own files. At the Massimo Group, we use the AVA behavioral assessment tool with our clients. That meant that I could use the raw profile results to look for patterns in teams. I was able to do that with the help of Ralph Spencer and Dave Borden. The results of that detailed analysis are in The Science of Teams.

Even if you don't like "scientific" reading, I urge you to read The Science of Teams section. I've tried to keep it as jargon-free as possible, and there are many insights that will help you either move to a teaming model or improve the way your current team works.

That background research helped me when I started interviewing commercial real estate teams. I talked with many more teams than I profiled in this book. I chose the teams for the book because they could teach some important lessons about teaming in commercial real estate.

I decided to use the basic definition of "team" as a starting point. *A team is a small group of people making a coordinated effort to reach a common goal.*

I studied teams only in commercial real estate. Sure, there are lessons to be learned from other kinds of teams, but the Massimo Group works with individuals, teams and firms in commercial real estate. I wanted the book to be relevant for our clients and people like them.

People use the word "team" very loosely, so I want to be clear about what I studied. I did not study people who work in the same office but who don't coordinate their efforts. I also chose not to study teams who coordinated their efforts for a single project or deal and then disbanded. I wanted to learn about the permanent teams that were popping up all over commercial real estate.

In the course of the research and interviews, I realized that many of these new teams were qualitatively different from many older forms of team. To describe this new kind of team, I adopted a term Craig Coppola used to describe his team: integrated team.

Integrated commercial real estate teams are built to dominate by creating structures, processes, policies and rituals that make the team more effective. Integrated teams build on the strengths of all team members and make their weaknesses irrelevant. On teams built to dominate, team members subordinate their personal goals to the team. The team's success becomes their success.

So, what have we learned about commercial real estate teams that are built to dominate? Let's start with why top producers are moving to integrated teaming.

WHY MOVE TO INTEGRATED TEAMS?

I've outlined the reasons we're seeing more and more integrated teams in commercial real estate. But you probably want to know the benefits for making the move to teaming. You want to know what's in it for you. That starts with income.

Being part of an integrated team can improve your overall income. If you're on the fulfillment side, you'll have the benefit of others with strong find and win skills generating the revenue. And what if you're a top producer? Then you get to do more of the things you do best, while you hand over other tasks to other team members.

Effective, integrated teams can find, win, and fulfill more business. The pie just gets bigger. There's another benefit, too. Because an integrated team can provide better service to clients, integrated teams have the possibility of more repeat business.

Being part of an integrated team will let you do more of the things you like to do and do well. At the Net Leased Investment Group, Parker Carroll made a conscious effort to divide the work so that every team member could do more of the things that he or she is good at.

Being part of an integrated team can improve your quality of life. Rick Canup warned Parker Carroll that while commercial real estate is a great way to make a living, you need a life outside of business, too. Before teaming up with Ari Harkov, Warner Lewis was very successful in business, but he found himself cancelling trips and other things he wanted to do because he was overwhelmed.

Becoming part of an integrated team let James Nelson take a vacation without being tethered to his cell phone 24/7.

The quality-of-life benefits aren't just outside the office. Being part of an integrated team can improve your quality of life at work. Over and over again, team members I interviewed mentioned loving their work and their teammates. If you love the work and the people you work with, you're far more likely to be successful. Quality of work life is good for retention, too. As Craig Coppola said, "If you spend your days doing what you truly love to do, and you make a lot of money, why would you ever leave?"

When there's camaraderie and great team spirit, team members will go the extra mile for each other and the team. There's no better example than the way Brent and Amy and the team at SVN-Miller pulled together when Super Storm Sandy hit. It took them only a few weeks to get their flooded and storm-ravaged office rebuilt.

Integrated teams are far more likely to secure and retain multi-location accounts. The demands of these valuable clients are one of the key forces driving a move to teams. Integrated teams are better at the fulfillment and servicing tasks that multi-location corporate accounts require. Several teams in this book work with multi-location clients, but Ashley-Hollis specializes in them. For an example of how they work, go back and look at their deal with Porsche Cars. It came only after more than a decade of relationship building and smaller deals. The project itself required constant communication with the client.

There are many good reasons that integrated teams are a good choice for leading commercial real estate professionals, among them increased income and a better quality of life at work and at home. Plus, the move to teams is being driven by some significant shifts in our business environment. So why isn't everyone jumping on the bandwagon?

WHY PEOPLE DON'T MOVE TO TEAMS

For several years I've been talking, intensely and intently, to all kinds of commercial real professionals about teams. A number of people have told me that they understood all the reasons switching to teams was a good idea, but they didn't think it was for them. They cited lots of reasons, which fell into four groups.

"I tried it and it didn't work." Maybe you got burned by a partner in the past. Maybe you trained juniors who left and took your clients with them. Maybe you felt like you were pulling the train and everyone else on the "team" was riding. Or, maybe you were a team member on a dysfunctional team. It's hard to overcome the emotional impact of a bad experience, but I hope you've learned some things from this book that will help you try again.

"We've never done it that way before." Some market researchers call this the "The Gravity of the Familiar." Human beings seem wired to want to stay with the familiar, even if there might be a better way. Think about the specific things that you don't like about the way you're doing business now. Many of them might be better in a team environment.

"I'm worried about giving up income or status or freedom." Those same market researchers call this "The Anxiety of the New Solution." We're wired to worry about things that are different, even if they might seem better. If you've succeeded in your career so far, you've mastered all kinds of new situations. You can handle a move to teaming if you decide to make it. And you'll never reap the positive benefits if you don't.

If you're considering a move to teaming, you want to think it through carefully. Ben Franklin came up with a way make difficult decisions that might help. He outlined his method in a letter to Joseph Priestly. Essentially, Franklin suggested dividing a sheet of paper down the middle to create two columns. Label one "Pros" or "Reasons to Move to Teaming" and the other "Cons" or "Reasons to Continue Doing Things the Old Way." Take a couple of days to enter reasons on both sides as you think of them. When you've gone a full day without adding anything new, look at your lists and make the decision that seems right. You'll find a lot in this book to help.

I've talked with people who know they want to move to teaming.

They think it's a good idea and that lots of benefits await them. Even so, they often have another reason for not making the move.

"I don't know how." You can know that teaming is the right thing for you and still not make the move if you don't know what to do. If you think back over the profile chapters, you'll realize that there's no one way to get from wherever you are now to teaming. So, there's no "best" first step. But there are things the most successful integrated teams do.

SOME THINGS THAT MOST OF THE TEAMS I STUDIED DID

Every team I studied is a unique team with a unique history and facing a unique situation. But most of them did the same things. You can do them, too.

Some of the things that our integrated teams did were not unique to integrated teams. They all had people who worked hard and had a "work hard" culture. So do lots of teams. They all paid close attention to their numbers. So do lots of teams. Those things seem to be table stakes for success in commercial real estate, whether you're an individual professional or a team.

Most teams had someone who took the lead. In most cases there was one person who got the team ball rolling. Cathy Jones and Jeff Mason both started their own firms. Craig Coppola waited until he had just the right junior. Brent Miller brought a whole office-full of people to his SVN-Miller team.

On most teams someone took a risk. Mark Hartum probably took the biggest risk, walking away from 95% of his business. But when Sam Hollis and Keith Ashley decided to partner up, Sam was the one with the book of business.

On most teams, compensation incentivizes team achievement and the alignment of individual goals with team goals. Bill Condon and Matt McGregor split everything evenly, no matter who originates a piece of business. Kyle Nagy gives extra bonus for community involvement and self-development. At Wosnack-Hartum, the principals work out a split for all deals in the next year and support staff get a salary plus a bonus tied to team achievement. Craig Coppola and Jeff Mason both talk about "incentivizing" the right behavior, but they do it in different ways.

Most teams are very careful about hiring. A bad hire can wreck a team. You want people with the right skills, the right personality for the role and the team, and the right work ethic. Anything less and you risk a fall-off in production at best and a complete team meltdown at worst. So our teams are careful about hiring, but they're not careful the same way. Multiple interviews, team interviews and the use of behavioral assessments like AVA are common. Harkov-Lewis has a fully structured process. Brent Miller has an informal process and compares hiring a new team member to adopting a child. Wosnack-Hartum outsources part of the process to a professional recruiter.

Most teams do not have virtual team members. In fact, only two of the teams, Cathy Jones' Investment Services Group and Parker Carroll's Net Leased Investment Group, have virtual members that they consider part of the team. In both cases the virtual team members make frequent and regular trips to the team office and use technology to stay in touch several times a day.

Most teams work side by side in some form of a bullpen. Teams built to dominate thrive on lots of easy communication, and that happens best when people work side by side. Teams with offices encourage open doors. Wosnack-Hartum has a special meeting area where team members can have a conversation that everyone can hear. The best description I've seen about why this works comes from the book Scaling Up Excellence by Robert Sutton and Huggy Rao of the Stanford Graduate School of Business:

> Michael Bloomberg strove to create such accountability during his long reign as mayor of New York City by jamming himself and his fifty-one most crucial staff members into a

"bullpen" that was the center of his administration—a small and often noisy room where the mayor sat in the center . Each resident sat in a small cubicle with a low partition. Everyone could see, and often hear, what everyone else was doing, and the burden to do the right thing—especially to support the sacred tenet of open communication—weighed heavily upon everyone in the room.

The authors conclude with this:

Jamming people close together is just one way to build an organization filled with people who can't escape relentless pressures to do the right thing, to live a mindset and hold others to it as well.

Most teams devote a lot of time and energy to review and transparency. Most have regular, scheduled meetings as well as project meetings. Harkov-Lewis even has a standup meeting with everyone every day. The frequent formal and informal communication, combined with an emphasis on transparency, helps assure that the right things are getting done in a timely manner. Teams that dominate have effective business processes.

Most teams pay attention to social support. Researchers on effective teaming note that top performing teams also provide social support for team members. Several teams have formal events designed to build strong relationships between team members. As you might expect, they do this in many different ways. Some have actual team-building events, like Team Nelson's learning to row a racing shell. Some teams have events where team members bring their spouses or families. CommCap does the opposite: They do something fun away from the office without family members. And SVN-Miller does community service where team members work together on a civic project like an annual river clean-up.

The teams have a common goal or shared vision. Different teams do this in various ways. The most formal and comprehensive is Team Nelson's Team Operating Agreement (TOA). It's a true team document, and it outlines goals and duties and the simple rules for how team members will deal with each other. Every team member signs it so they can see what's expected of them and every other team member, and to signify their commitment to doing their part. If you haven't done so already, go back to the Team Nelson chapter and make sure you access the download of the Team Operating Agreement.

Those are common things that teams built to dominate do. On most items there's a good deal of variation on the ways to get things done. So you have lots of options, but there are some things that we know for sure.

SOME THINGS WE KNOW FOR SURE

Great teams don't happen by accident. You can create a team built to dominate if you pay attention to what teams built to dominate, like the ones in this book, do. That gives you a lot of leeway to adjust things to your unique situation. But there's a catch.

Great teams are a system. God may be in the details, but the details aren't enough. Great teams are a system. You have to have all the key themes, and they must reinforce each other.

Think about the air conditioning system in your car. There are lots of parts. There's a condenser and a fan and a thermostat and hoses and vents. For the system to work, you have to have all of the parts and they must be able to work together. Teams built to dominate are the same. Take a look at the diagram I shared with you in the Introduction:

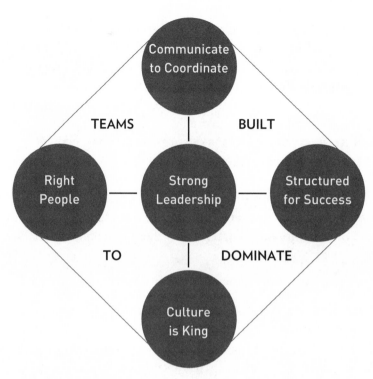

The 5 Themes of Commercial Real Estate Teams
Built to Dominate

Teams built to dominate have all of the five themes working and working together. All of the themes affect each other. You can make the themes work in a variety of different ways as we've seen when we looked at what most of the teams we studied did. What you can't do is forget about one of the themes.

You can create a team built to dominate if you do all of the five themes well and if you coordinate them so they each make the others better. One reason that teams built to dominate are rare is that it takes work and effort to keep all five themes working together.

Teams built to dominate are also rare because they require everyone on the team to have the right kind of ambition. The right kind of ambition puts the success of the team above personal ambition. Team members can trust each other when they know that every team member is putting the team first.

The bottom line is this: It takes hard work and constant vigilance to build a team that will dominate, and then it takes even more to keep things working well. Sometimes luck has a role, too. It's not easy to build a commercial real estate team to dominate, but it's worth it.

Now it's your turn. Here are two different action steps. If you do not have a team, the first one gives you things you can do right now to begin to build one. If you already have a team, skip to the second action step.

ACTION STEPS FOR BUILDING A TEAM THAT DOMINATES

If you want to build a team that dominates, there may be a lot to do. Here are a few ideas to get you started.

- Outline everything you do on a daily basis and identify your core strengths and your most productive activities.
- Identify items that are not truly productive, that have a direct negative impact on your generating income.
- Initially outsource/delegate as many of those items as you can. This will be uncomfortable initially and will require capital, but this is really an investment in your personal growth.
- Look for others in your office or in your market, even competitive colleagues who have complementary skill sets and have your same level of work ethic.
- On your own, or with a potential team member, outline a vision for where you want your business to go, and draft some ideas on how this will be achieved.

ACTION STEPS FOR IMPROVING AN EXISTING TEAM

- Review everything—all five themes.
- Review your team vision; if you don't have one, create one, as a team.
- Review the job descriptions for each position the team. If you do not have these, outline the roles and responsibilities of each position.

- Complete a Team Operating Agreement confirming the goals, roles and responsibility of each team member—leverage the Team Operating Agreement form in this book's downloadable content.
- Review team compensation and incentives; confirm they support the team vision.
- Identify the bottlenecks in your team's transaction process.
- Potentially complete an AVA personality assessment for each member of the team (review The Science of Teams chapter for more information on the AVA).
- Commit to a weekly meeting at the same time, on the same day, with no exceptions.
- Identify a meeting champion to coordinate the agenda items with each team member.
- Team meetings should incorporate a review, an accountability segment, open discussions and established targets for the week.

———————•———————

Congratulations, you have read some, if not all, of the profiles in this book. If you followed my suggestion of using a pen and highlighter, your book and/or eBook should have scores or hundreds of notes and ideas. Guess what? You are only partially there. This next chapter— The Science of Teams—will provide you with at least as many ideas and insights on how to structure your own dominant team. Don't make the mistake of simply skimming this content. Truly dominant teams are not created by happenstance. Herein lies the rest of your playbook; study it well.

THE SCIENCE OF TEAMS

Meeting Today's Client Expectations

Even before I started identifying and interviewing commercial real estate teams for this book, I wanted to find out what science says about teams and about what makes great ones great. After all, psychologists and anthropologists and many other kinds of scientists have conducted tons of research into the subject. One of the first things I discovered was that an awful lot of the research simply didn't apply to the teams I wanted to study.

ACADEMIC STUDIES DON'T ADDRESS COMMERCIAL REAL ESTATE TEAMS

I wanted to understand the integrated teams that were beginning to appear more and more in the commercial real estate industry. They were a new way of doing business, built for the long haul, and solving real challenges in the marketplace.

Unfortunately, most of the academic studies of teams were irrelevant for this book. They were laboratory experiments where researchers brought together a group of people, usually students or volunteers, gave them an artificial task and drew conclusions from what happened.

That might be fine for an academic paper, but it doesn't tell us anything about ongoing, operational teams solving problems in the real world. There was also another kind of research we couldn't use.

Many of the real world studies of teams analyzed product

development teams or project teams, or operational teams that exist in a matrix environment. Those teams form for a single purpose, achieve their goal, and disband. The commercial real estate teams I studied were built to last a long time, which made their team-culture challenges very different.

There was some helpful research, though. "How to Manage Virtual Teams" by Frank Siebdrat, Martin Hoegl and Holger Ernst in the Sloan Management Review is an example. The title refers to virtual teams, but the article includes lots of good stuff for co-located teams like the integrated commercial real estate teams. The researchers identified two kinds of processes that help make permanent, operational teams effective.

In general, team processes can be classified into two categories: task-related—including those that help ensure each member is contributing fully; and socio-emotional—including those that increase the cohesion of the group.

Sure enough, the integrated commercial real estate teams use both kinds of processes. They use task-related processes, including meetings, formal procedures and communication rituals to help make team members more productive. And they all had regular ways to provide social support for each other and the team as a whole. Those insights helped shape the things I watched for when I interviewed scores of teams, but there was one insight from the scientific researchers that I blew off at first. They put it this way: "Don't underestimate the significance of small distances."

They meant that having people work side by side in the same space makes for more effective teaming, and any departure from that degrades performance. A Microsoft study elaborated on that point.

When team members don't sit together they tend to replace easy verbal exchanges with harder and more formal conversations. Rather than quick, efficient discussions about small, tactical decisions, subjects queue up and wait to be discussed later. Often, later never comes.

I thought that was nuts. After all, we hear so much about virtual teams and teleworking. I expected that top-performing teams would have lots of virtual team members. So I asked everyone I interviewed how many virtual, full-time team members they had. In all but two cases the answer was zero, none. In both of the teams with virtual team members, those team members regularly and physically came into the office to either attend meetings or simply re-connect.

Our dominant, integrated commercial real estate teams do leverage virtual support people, but they're not part of the team; instead, they support the team or a single team member. They aren't in the workflow of the task-related processes. They don't participate in most of the activities that provide social support for team members.

The academic research on real world, operational teams tells us that dominant teams use processes to drive both performance and social support. Both of those are important. Task-oriented processes keep the work on track and up to standard. Social support encourages buy-in, commitment and engagement. You need both types if you want to build a team that dominates for a long time.

RELEVANT APPLICATION

Academic research gives us lessons about the processes that make for a top performing team. That's only part of the equation. I wanted to learn what mix of people you need to have the best possible team. For that I brought in Ralph Spencer to assist me with the analysis and interpretation of the teams we profiled in this book and also those we have coached and consulted with since the inception of the Massimo Group. Ralph is a leading consultant and trainer in the industry. I am proud to call him a colleague and, more importantly, my friend. Additionally we consulted with Dave Borden, President of Bizet Human Asset Management. Together we looked at old style and new style commercial real estate teams through the lens of Activity Vector Analysis (AVA).

There are several analysis and profiling instruments out there today. Like many other assessments, including DiSC, Myers-Briggs, and others, AVA is based on psychological research that was completed in the early 20th century. In 1948, pioneering psychologist William V. Clarke introduced the first AVA assessment.

The AVA is used internationally and is EEOC compliant as a valid and reliable natural behaviors assessment. The basic instrument has been fine-tuned several times to maintain its reliability and validity. Most of the changes have been in the words used to describe traits. For example, some words have a different connotation today from when AVA was first introduced.

Worldwide, companies and consulting firms, as well as professional sports teams, use AVA to help them make better decisions about people. They use AVA in hiring and assignment decisions to fill jobs with people who are most likely to succeed. And they use AVA in career counseling and coaching to help individuals improve performance.

At the Massimo Group, all our clients complete the AVA. We chose it from the many instruments available because it's been validated by decades of research and use and it's easy to use and understand.

If you would like to complete an AVA for yourself or your entire team, contact us by visiting **www.massimo-group.com/contact**

We worked with Ralph Spencer to develop customized reporting for the commercial real estate industry. We have profiled top-producing agents across North America and have continued to evolve our platform over the years. AVA evaluates people on four dimensions or vectors that assess a person's behavioral tendencies:

> *Assertiveness* is the tendency to take risks and engage the unknown to accomplish a goal or objective. People with low assertiveness are more likely to be service-oriented and may tend to be more cautious and passive. Those high in assertiveness may tend to be direct and demanding.

> *Sociability* is the tendency to be with or around people. People low in sociability may tend to be analytical and introspective, while those high in sociability may tend to be extroverted.

Calmness is the tendency to remain calm and patient. People who are high in calmness tend to be controlled and patient. Those low in calmness tend to be impatient, more deadline oriented and responsive.

Conformity is the tendency to follow the rules or protocol and to avoid failure or making a mistake. People high in conformity may exhibit perfectionistic behavior and tend to be detail oriented. They want to avoid personal censure. When they are unsure how to proceed, they look outside for guidance about how to do things. Those low in conformity will tend to be more independent and self-reliant.

Please note; for the purposes of this book we will only present the initial levels of analysis of the AVA tool. This tool is much more detailed and provides an incredible amount of information that takes expert analysis to truly understand. With the help of Ralph and Dave, we have done this. The results for each of the four vectors presented range from 1 to 9. In the case of the AVA model, the aggregate of the four vectors must equal 20 points. As we will demonstrate, these four vectors will create a "Pattern." The pattern shape is used to describe the relative strength of each vector compared to the other vectors. While sometimes we will speak about an individual vector, it is always the integration of all four vectors that determines an individual's natural behaviors.

AVA is a very sophisticated instrument, and it requires special training to understand why it works in detail. I'm presenting our findings in a simplified manner to keep this chapter readable and to make the lessons easier to digest and, more importantly, to implement. The following is full graphical representation template for AVA Results. We have simplified the remaining graphs in this chapter for ease of interpretation.

ASSERTIVENESS

ASSERTIVENESS
The tendency to take risks and engage the unknown to accomplish a goal or objective

LOW	1	2	3	4	5	6	7	8	9	HIGH
	passive		reactive	situational assertive			assertive		driving nature	

Cautious / Conservative / Helpful / Steady Trustful / Modest / Passive

Results Oriented / Decisive / Demanding Take Charge / Direct / Forceful

SOCIABILITY

SOCIABILITY
The tendency to be with and around people

LOW	1	2	3	4	5	6	7	8	9	HIGH
	reserved		congenial	situational outgoing			sociable		highly social	

Seeks Privacy / Working Alone / Analysis / Skeptical Reserved / Serious / Introspective/Reflective

Extroverted/ People Acceptance / Persuasive / Visibility Optimistic / Friendly / Outgoing

CALMNESS

CALMNESS
The tendency to remain calm and patient and to avoid situations involving unexpected change

LOW	1	2	3	4	5	6	7	8	9	HIGH
	restless, impatient		animated	situational paced			patient & controlled		relaxed, calm	

Impatient / Constant Change / Time Sensitive / Variety / Fast Paced / Deadline Oriented / Natural Multi-Tasking

Patient / Tolerant / Consistent / Quality Oriented Tranquil / Unemotional / Prefers the Unknown

CONFORMITY

CONFORMITY
The tendency to follow the rules or protocol and to avoid failure or making a mistake.

LOW	1	2	3	4	5	6	7	8	9	HIGH
	highly independent		independent	situational independent or conforming			obedient, cooperative		conforming	

Self Reliance / Free to Act / Big Picture Individualistic / Opinionated / Independent

Perfectionist / Precise & Detail Oriented / Structure Needs Feedback / Conforming / Cooperative

Graphical Representation Template for AVA Results

What follows is an analysis of dominant teams, from a natural behavior standpoint. This approach allows us to evaluate teams based on individual roles, responsibilities, and personalities. Significant external factors impact team performance, such as the team's environment (corporate, national firm, independent), as well as the individual's Knowledge, Attitude, Skills and Habits (or "KASH," as Ralph would say). This chapter will touch on these external factors. However, the focus and supported findings will highlight the key impact of the personalities of individual team members and their roles and responsibilities on team performance.

THE INDIVIDUAL PROFILE–TOP PRODUCERS

Following is a chart demonstrating the profile for typical "top producers" in commercial real estate. Those top producers tend to be highly "assertive." This implies they are likely results-oriented and direct. In the commission-based practice of commercial real estate, they are focused on getting deals completed. They are also situationally "social," meaning they are likely able to be social when needed but they don't have to be the center of attention. You generally won't find them in the back corner of a networking session, but you won't necessarily find them in the middle of the room leading a company cheer, either. Top producers are typically low in "calmness"; not a big surprise here. They tend to be responsive, seek constant change and be fast-paced. Finally, they tend to be low in "conformity." They are likely self-reliant, individualistic and independent. For example, you will not typically find these folks as non-executive staff on a Fortune 500 company or as an employee in a hierarchical organization like a public CPA firm. If they are in those situations, they are most likely expending a lot of emotional energy to perform well in their roles.

After working with hundreds of top producers across North America, we have identified the individual commercial real estate "Top Producer" AVA pattern shape, or profile, is **9-6-3-2**. Historically, the nature of the commercial real estate environment, including straight commission, has rewarded producers with this profile. These are people who are generally able to make decisions more rapidly, are persuasive and are able to find, win and fulfill business.

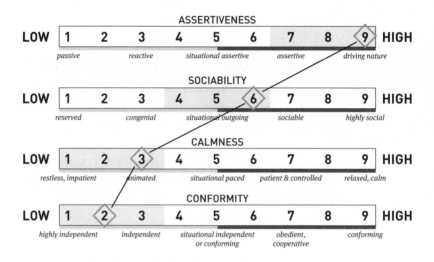

Ideal individual profile for a
top commercial real estate producer

Remember that AVA is structured so that the total score for all four vectors must be 20. That means that if some vectors, like assertiveness or sociability, are high, the other vectors must be low, and vice versa.

It is also very important to note that not all top producers fit this exact profile. We have worked with many commercial real estate professionals who do not match all four of these vectors, yet they are very successful in their careers. However, through our coaching experience of working with hundreds of clients, I can absolutely share with you that those with low assertiveness are generally challenged to prospect effectively, to find new opportunities; so we focus on these issues. Likewise, those with low sociability generally will not easily engage in personal presence activities. When we coach people like this, we usually focus on physical and digital efforts to create a greater presence.

People's behavior generally doesn't change. In some cases, significant events in someone's life may force them to look at the world differently, but usually an individual's self-concept will remain relatively the same. Coaching can help people succeed without changing their underlying self-concept. We know that people can develop behavioral modifications to overcome some of their natural tendencies that can get in the way of achieving success.

We have identified profiles for those who are strong at winning the business and those who are strong at fulfilling the business. There are proven profiles for team members based on their specific role, as well as who they will be working with. Putting a dominant team together is not based on "gut feel." A truly dominant team consists of individuals who are self-aware of their natural behaviors and excel, naturally, at the role they fill on the team. On a dominant team, the different personalities mesh to enable more effective communication and thus, greater levels of trust, and ultimately production.

Once you understand individual AVA profiles, you can analyze why dominant teams work so well.

INDUSTRY TRENDS AND IMPACT ON THE FORMATION OF TEAMS

In the Introduction, I outlined our industry is moving toward multi-location representation, and/or towards more sophisticated sellers or landlords, which is the institutionalization of commercial real estate. As we move in this direction, clients no longer highly value the independent, do-it-all cowboy the way they once did.

For more on this, I asked Ralph Spencer to provide additional industry insight. Here is what he says about the client expectations for today's commercial real estate professionals:

There is a point where the top dog is not going to stay the top dog unless he/she figures out how to deliver a higher overall level of service to the clients. It's very difficult to win significant assignments. It's a challenge to deal with the larger companies and more established owners and users as an individual.

What are you, Superman? You've got to have some additional people at the table when you're trying to win the business. And the truth is, you've got to have more people at the table when you service the business.

I think most of today's teams are convenient associations, but I believe we're seeing the evolution of teams in the industry. The first set of teams was associate teams that complement each other. However, the industry is quickly recognizing that the client is demanding a high level of service for their needs. The individual alone simply cannot get the job done. Ultimately, that is where clients will look for, fully integrated teams. But right now what we have, for the most part, are structured, collaborative teams.

They agree to collaborate, cooperate, divide the pie, have a strategy, and have responsibilities that each of them fulfill, because they recognize that if they do that, everyone can do better. We've also got some rainmakers who recognize that, "I'm running myself crazy. I can't do it all. So I'm going to get some other players to come in and help." That way the rainmaker can do more of what he or she does best and get other people to do the rest.

The second thing that's happening is you've got to have a little more structure to succeed today. You just can't wake up in the morning and say "what am I going to do today?" And you have to be able to provide a much wider range of services to clients and do so with expertise at all service levels. But the problem is, an individual, or even a team made up of convenient associations, can't deliver what's needed. They don't make people who can do it all. Because when one vector on the AVA moves up, another must move down. And the guy who's going to win the business is almost always going to be high on assertiveness and/or sociability.

This individual broker, top dog, is generally an outgoing, people person. They tend to be highly animated, entertaining, and restless. They're also self-reliant cowboys. The problem is that this model is just not a teaming model, and it's not a high servicing model. I'm not saying that an assertive person can't be a team player, but when you add a commission component to it, you eat what you kill, and particularly if they're not very social it's very difficult for them to team. And if they do team, they say, "I get it all, and I'll give you something, maybe." So that's a challenge.

The next thing that's evolving, is the customer's saying, "we're getting ready to give you X thousands of dollars in commissions and you don't return our calls. You're not available when we need you. You're not showing the property— you're not paying attention to the details. You said you were going to do this lease analysis."

And what that's doing is pushing up the needs for higher calmness and conformity, providing higher service levels with greater structure and accountability. The individual "cowboy" brokers can't just be blowing and going; they've got to have some consistency. Clients demand it.

The "best guy," the individual top producer, doesn't have the total composition of natural behaviors to fully and truly provide the level of service that is demanded today. No one does. The business is changing, and you need to provide an expanded level of service, a deeper level of service. You need to be much more flexible, and one person cannot meet all of today's client demands.

No one individual is highly assertive, highly social, highly calm and highly structured. Remember, no one can have a total score of more than 20. And today's assignments demand a high degree in each of these four vectors. As Ralph states, one person cannot meet all the client's enhanced needs and expectations.

Before we move forward, I wanted to share some insight from Dave Borden. Again, Dave works with major corporations, sports teams and private companies, assisting them with their problematic team structures. Dave reflects on why most teams are not "true" teams:

> We always talk about teams that are too much alike and the difficulties that develop when teams are too much alike, not only on the limitation they have in how they perform, because they're missing other things, but also the difficulties they may have in working together because they are too much alike.
>
> A large group of assertive people working together may have difficulty getting to decisions that everyone buys into. Teams that have everyone that's high in sociability may have difficulties because they're all competing for attention. Teams that are very high in calmness may have problems as a team because they can't move to decisions because they just can't go very fast. And teams that are high in conformity have difficulties because the team by nature will develop a fear of making a mistake. And if they're in areas that are new to them and they can't find information, they will simply stop. They will be lost.
>
> So that's when the team members are alike. When there are opposite team member behaviors involved, either one or a few, you have to make sure that the natural tendency to dislike their opposite doesn't create ineffectiveness on the team. It can create silos in the organization down beneath them.
>
> When team members recognize and value their differences (and that has to happen by not only understanding the other person but also understanding yourself and the shortcomings you have, primarily when you over-apply your strengths) they have to work from that direction to make sure that the team understands and functions well with those differences.
>
> The teams that normally operate best are those that recognize their differences. They're the teams that not only develop the best decisions, but they also don't get to the market too slow or too fast. You want to get to the market, like when I was at Black & Decker in the consumer business, before your competitors do, but you also want to make sure that you get the second sale.

But you don't want to spend so much time hemming and hawing on quality that you get to the market with a great product but find your competitor was there 2 months before. So balancing the behaviors in a positive way can lead to the real high-performing teams that do everything, not only from the sale side but from the problem-solving side to the execution side and the support side.

It could be they're too much alike. We have people who don't get along with others because they're too much alike. And we have people who don't get along with others because they're not alike. And in both situations, both players have to understand what behavioral modifications they would have to make to work together.

THE CRE BUSINESS CONTINUUM AND IMPACT ON TEAMS

Individual producers understand the basic business continuum. You need to find business, win the business and fulfill the business, and do so continually or your pipeline will shut down. It amazes me how many folks will call us and tell us they had a "Great 2nd quarter!" followed by "And now I have nothing in the pipeline." As I will share, given the natural tendencies required by each of these three stages of the continuum, independent commercial real estate professionals generally are not strong in each of these essential elements of the business. As such, not only do they suffer, but their clients suffer as well.

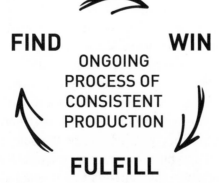

The Commercial Real Estate Business Continuum

You can understand why it is so important to match these three basic, essential components and the natural behaviors that best fit each stage. From here you can better appreciate the basic needs of a team and start to design a team that can be in position to secure a consistent flow of high-quality opportunities. They can be in position to dominate their competition.

Let's look at each stage separately.

Find. Finding business means prospecting, which requires you to "STP" (see the people), network, connect, uncover the opportunities, etc. You've got to be social and outgoing to pick up the phone, go to networking sessions and ask for business.

This is what Dave Borden calls the "core passion." You're high in assertiveness and sociability, which typically makes you move toward people and move toward a goal. You're generally low in calmness. As soon as one thing is done, you start on something else. And you're very independent and toward the low end of the conformity vector. That's going to allow you, when you do prospect, to be very comfortable. You will come across as credible and persuasive.

There are always exceptions; but, generally speaking, if you are going to be out finding business, you are going to be seeing and connecting with people and you are going to be at least midlevel to high in sociability. This brings us to the win stage.

Win. Winning the business means you are securing the listing, tenant/buyer rep, financing, management or consulting agreement. You are likely highly assertive but also are at least midlevel on sociability. You are likely less conforming and more independent and self-reliant. You see a "no" as a temporary obstacle.

Some people have to be trained to ask for the sale. Those higher on the conformity vector are more likely to be structured. No matter how much training they get, asking for the sale and positioning themselves to win the business is a challenge for them and takes a lot of effort. They tend to be inhibited by a fear of failure. To them, a no is a no. And they don't want that.

Fulfill. Once the assignment is secured, it needs to be serviced and ultimately closed. A higher level of structure and detail is required when compared to initially finding and winning the business. Now you have to coordinate the team and the projects, all while keeping the client informed.

Fulfillment has always been important. Three things have changed. First, fulfillment has become more complex and more comprehensive. At the same time, due diligence and deal facilitation have become more important. There are more multi-location client opportunities than ever. Those things mean the due diligence, maintenance and fulfillment functions require people with higher skill levels than you might have needed 20 years ago.

Naturally those who excel in this role tend to be mid to lower in assertiveness and higher in conformity. More likely, they are going to take direction and want to perform, especially when they have a little higher calmness. They're going to be friendly, but they're also going to be very helpful.

You would also want someone who is generally calm. The client will demand somebody who is service oriented or someone who's there and is going to make sure at the end that everything is done right. And that would typically be found in someone high in conformity. The industry is changing and the details do matter, so consider having someone on your team who is detail oriented.

The person who is good at today's fulfillment functions would tend to be higher in calmness and conformity. That does not mean top producers couldn't learn to handle the due diligence and fulfillment parts of the job. They certainly could. Anyone could learn how to handle the fulfillment role.

What's important is that some people have a set of natural behaviors that are better aligned with the role and the associated responsibilities. It will generally be easier for them to excel at the position and sustain a high, consistent level of work product. People who are not a good natural fit for the work will be able to do it, but will likely expend a lot of effort in the process.

DISSECTING DOMINANT TEAMS

By now you should understand the basic concepts of the AVA tool, its application, and its limitations. I also shared with you how this tool can help you assemble a strong, client-focused team. Now I want to go a step further and explain how AVA can help us understand why dominant teams work the way they do.

It is worth repeating: The AVA tool is much more detailed and provides an incredible amount of information that takes expert analysis to truly understand. The findings here are accurate but simplified to keep this chapter readable and the lessons easier to digest and, more importantly, to implement.

In addition to those teams profiled in the book and a few which I noted as being clients, we have had the pleasure of working with many top producing, dominant teams throughout North America. As such, we have many examples of team structure and composition that will help you better understand the impact of matching the right personalities with the right roles and responsibilities and doing so in a way that creates effective communication and ultimately enhances production.

Don't focus on the number of team members on the examples provided. For example, if you have a team of five, you will gain tremendous insight from reviewing the examples of teams of three, as much as you would by evaluating a team of five or more.

For confidentiality purposes I have removed all names and unique identifying details of the teams whose profiles we are sharing. Let's start with a very common team structure; a partnership with an administrator.

THE PARTNERSHIP WITH ASSISTANT TEAM

Below you will find the pattern of a three person team. The two partners' profiles are represented by the square and the circle. The admin/support person profile is represented by the triangle. We will use the triangle symbol to represent support staff/admin for every team we analyze.

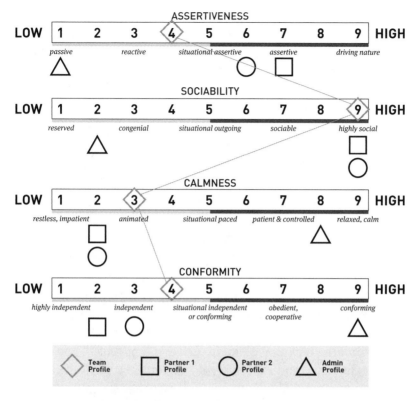

ASSERTIVENESS

LOW	1	2	3	4	5	6	7	8	9	HIGH

passive   *reactive*   *situational assertive*   *assertive*   *driving nature*

SOCIABILITY

LOW	1	2	3	4	5	6	7	8	9	HIGH

reserved   *congenial*   *situational outgoing*   *sociable*   *highly social*

CALMNESS

LOW	1	2	3	4	5	6	7	8	9	HIGH

restless, impatient   *animated*   *situational paced*   *patient & controlled*   *relaxed, calm*

CONFORMITY

LOW	1	2	3	4	5	6	7	8	9	HIGH

highly independent   *independent*   *situational independent or conforming*   *obedient, cooperative*   *conforming*

◇ Team Profile   ☐ Partner 1 Profile   ○ Partner 2 Profile   △ Admin Profile

Team profile for a partnership with assistant

These three personalities, when combined, create a "team profile" of **4-9-3-4**, as represented by the diamonds. Understanding the AVA, you may conclude this is not a very assertive team. The assertiveness rating of 4 suggests the team is situationally assertive. But don't forget the two partners, as represented by the square and circle, exhibit tendencies to be more assertive. In fact, their respective profiles show high tendencies toward assertiveness (6 and 7, respectively). Their administrator's assertiveness is 1. In this case, the administrator is not assertive at all; she is typically cautious and conservative. However, this plays well with the partners' higher degrees of assertiveness. These opposite profiles continue throughout the AVA model. The partners are generally social, whereas their administrator is naturally not. The partners are generally not very calm, nor very structured, whereas the administrator tends to be both highly calm and highly structured.

Remember what Dave Borden explained earlier in this chapter? Having a team of all highly assertive people will be very competitive, but ultimately little will get done. Both partners, individually, are solid producers; but without the administrator, this team would suffer as deals would not be completed as quickly nor as correctly.

Let me share with you some personal knowledge about this team. The two partners are focused on finding and winning the business. They do what they say they're going to do, they want to be liked, and they are. Each is very personable. Their administrator is quiet and reserved, but she is going to make sure everything is done on time and correctly. She's going to support the heck out of it.

Deeper analysis of the AVA also tells us that the administrator adjusts her natural behaviors to keep pace with the two partners, but not so much that it becomes problematic and unsustainable. (Sorry, I promise, I won't go in to "deep analysis" mode again.) Remember, the focus is on the personalities. Culturally, all three tend to be focused on providing a high degree of work product and understand the meaning of going above and beyond. They go at it in different ways, and they're very complementary. All three team members understand their strengths, what they do well and what they need to do to make the team successful.

Again, the "team profile" is **4-9-3-4**. This would suggest the team is situationally assertive (4). Given that they focus on key client relationships and multi-locational opportunities, this makes sense. The team is generally very social (9). The key client relationships and the retention and expansion of these relationships come more naturally. The team tends to be low in calmness (3), suggesting they are reactive and fast paced. Every member of this team understands what it means to work hard. Finally, this team is situationally independent (4). This is highly impacted by the administrator's tendency to be very structured. (Her conformity is a 9.)

THE SENIOR, JUNIOR, ASSISTANT TEAM

Now let's look at another three-person team. In this case, the two producers have a senior-junior relationship. In addition, you will see that their administrative assistant has a significantly different profile from that of the assistant outlined in the previous team above: **1-9-4-6** compared to a **1-2-8-9**. Yes, both are generally very cautious and conservative naturally, but that's where the similarities end.

This West Coast-based team is a boutique team and not affiliated with a national organization. Yet they are profoundly successful and seen as experts in their niche, on not only a local level, but national as well.

Their team diagram is as follows:

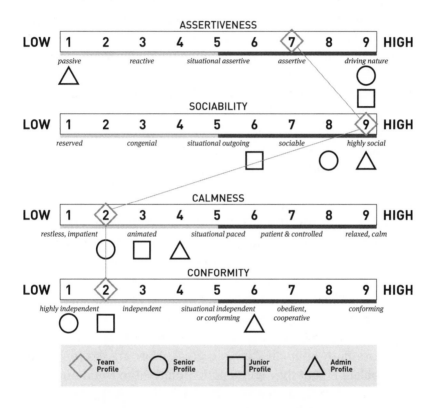

Team profile for a senior, junior and assistant.

These three personalities, when combined, create a team profile of **7-9-2-2**. This team has stronger tendencies in both assertiveness and sociability than the prior three-person team that we studied. Is this "better"? Not necessarily. It's just different. This team profile also supports the find, win, fulfill business model outlined earlier in this chapter.

So, let's break down these individual personalities to understand why this team works so well. The senior and junior are very similar. In this case, the senior broker is represented by the circle (9-8-2-1) and the junior broker is represented by the square (9-6-3-2). Both are hunters, strong in finding business. Adding the senior's high sociability (8), the team also enjoys entertaining clients and crafting strong relationships, which, in their field of tenant and landlord representation, is very important. However, neither the senior nor junior exhibits a "service-oriented behavior." Yes, they love the hunt and the kill, but don't ask them to prepare the meal.

This is where their administrator's natural behaviors enhance the team and the team's culture. Like the two producers, the admin/support person is generally social (9). This is a fun team; they enjoy working together. However, they also understand the demands of working hard. The admin/support person's profile results in a 1 for assertiveness. She is generally steady and cautious, which plays off so well to the two producers' vector 1 results (both 9s). However, her calmness is a 4. She can generally keep pace with this team. Remember from the first profile, the admin/support calmness was an 8. I shared with you how she adjusts to keep pace. This adjustment takes more energy for the other administrator than the administrator profiled with this current team. (Heck, I promised I wouldn't go "deep," but I did! Okay, I won't let that happen again.)

The admin/support person is the glue that holds this team together. She is mission critical for them because the senior and junior are both hunters. They are great. They are a strong pair. The problem is that they will tend to promise the world and they will get more excited about going and finding the new client to develop than they ever will about fulfilling their promises and representations. That's not a problem, because their administrator is positioned to help.

SENIOR, JUNIOR, ASSOCIATE, ADMIN TEAM
It's time to move up a notch and examine a dominant team of four members. For that we will review a team that works with

a national company and completes investment deals all across the country.

Their team diagram is as follows:

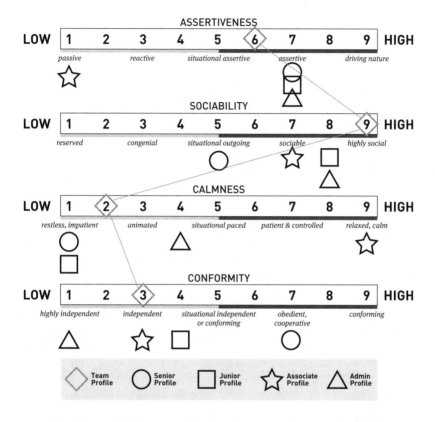

Team profile for a senior, junior, associate and admin

These four individual personalities, when combined, create a team profile of **6-9-2-3**. When this team approaches situations, they're going to be generally assertive but confident in their approach. The team pattern shows assertiveness at 6 and conformity of 3. Also, they are typically going to be more credible and, because of their sociability (9), be able to reach out to people, communicate their thoughts and present a persuasive style.

The senior on this team is represented by the circle **(7-5-1-7)** and is responsible for finding business. He is relatively high assertive and moderately social. Since most of his clients are located outside of his market, this actually works well for him; most of his client interaction is on the telephone and not in person.

The junior producer is represented by the square (**7-8-1-4**). He too has a similar role of prospecting for business, and the senior and junior work together to pursue opportunities. Yes, they are different in age, but their personalities work well when focused on their responsibilities of prospecting.

The admin/support person is represented by the triangle. In this case, the administrator plays more the role of a marketing assistant. In fact, his profile is more in line with what we see with a typical producer (**7-8-4-1**) than a support person, and ultimately this may be a better fit as the team continues to evolve. This is a key point.

Given the first three profiles, it is obvious that more of a service-oriented personality is required to make this a dominant team. This is where the fourth member fits. She is the "fulfiller," and is represented by the star on the chart. Her role is to service the business that the senior and junior procure. Her profile is **1-7-9-3**. She is typical social (7). She fits within the culture of the team, yet she is generally patient and consistent (calmness 9). From this profile, we can assume this is a reactive person. She tends to wait to be told what to do. Again, this fits very well with the role. She is generally easy to get along with (sociability 7), which is what we want in those interacting with clients during the fulfillment stage.

THE SERVICE-ORIENTED TEAM—NATIONAL ACCOUNT MANAGEMENT/CORPORATE ENVIRONMENTS

So far we have examined "self-sustaining teams," teams that, regardless of their environment—whether a boutique company, a regional firm or international commercial real estate organization—have the ability to find, win and fulfill business. These teams could leave their national affiliations and still dominate. Likewise, the boutique teams would continue to lead if they ever decide to align with a national firm. They are just built that way.

But what about teams that work more in the corporate and institutional real estate environments? Certainly accounts need to be secured, but the focus on these accounts is to service them; to assist them with multi-locational opportunities.

We work with such a team. They are affiliated with a major international commercial real estate organization and focus on tenant representation. This team works with some of the biggest accounts in the country. They are a dominant team. But like all dominant teams, they are also looking to enhance their production and ultimately improve service to their clients.

In this team profile I will share the initial team composition, which was strong in its own right, and then the team composition, based on adding an identified need.

The initial team profile was as outlined as follows:

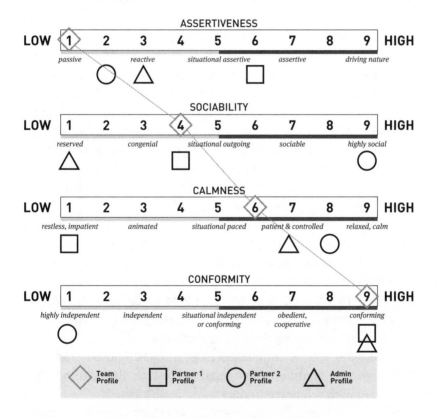

**Team profile for a service-oriented team,
before adding the new hire**

You should notice right away that this team composite profile is significantly different from those we have presented previously. The team profile is **1-4-6-9**. This profile suggests the team has tendencies to be helpful, somewhat social, cautious, relatively calm and highly structured and by-the-book. This is what you want in a service-oriented team.

This Midwest-based team consists two equal partners and an administrative person. The partners are represented by the circle and square and the administrator by the triangle. Notice the patterns of the partners. They are dissimilar in all four vectors. They are opposites in personalities. They have been working together for over 20 years, and, based on their profiles, they act like an old married couple. In actuality, they aren't married; but if you have been married for more than 10 years, you will know what your partner is thinking, how they will react and how you can best communicate. In addition, you will also know what buttons not to push!

Their assistant **(3-1-7-9)** is a behind-the-scenes person. Her profile suggests that she is generally cautious, introverted, calm and structured. Ideally, she will not be interacting with clients but is a perfect personality for providing consistent service and conducting fulfillment activities.

As long as this team focuses on account services or internal account servicing (as with a corporate real estate department) they will continue to flourish. This team can rely on company referrals and/or their existing client growth.

However, let's assume this is not an internal commercial real estate, corporate team. In this case, there is always a risk that major accounts could move elsewhere. Then the lack of a strong account-procurement element could be disastrous. Putting it another way, if you took this team and dropped them in a different city, without the umbrella of a major institution's referring deals to them, they would be in trouble. Again, this is service team. A purely service-oriented team will be challenged to go out and find business, but in the evolving world of commercial real estate, they can be quite successful in the right environment.

Yes, as noted earlier in this chapter, the industry is moving toward account servicing; and this is where dominant, self-sustaining teams have evolved—on the service side, on the fulfillment side.

The service-oriented team profiled here recognized the opportunity for business enhancement. Like all dominant teams, and even those individuals who want more from their commercial real estate careers, they are always asking, "How can we/I get better?" They asked if there was a better personality fit for their team. They wanted to find someone who, along with proven experience, had the natural behaviors for prospecting; someone to go out and get more business.

And that's what they did. Through a finely tuned recruitment and evaluation process, including the use of the AVA tool, they added a new associate, represented by the star. This associate (9-8-2-1) was given the sole responsibility to find new business for this proven service-oriented team. This one new hire changed the team composition significantly, as shown here:

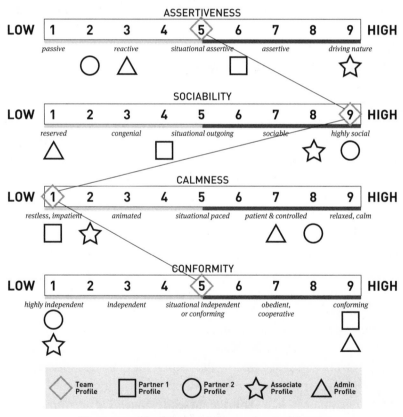

Team profile for a service-oriented team,
after adding the new hire

The new team profile is **5-9-1-5**. Remember, the original team profile was **1-4-6-9**. Thus, from a purely natural behavior perspective, the team now has a greater tendency to be more assertive (moved from a 1 to a 6), more social (moved from a 4 to a 9), less calm and thus more responsive (moved from a 6 to a 1) and less structured (moved from a 9 to a 5). Again, the individual team members are still in place to service the business, but now the team is also better structured to find and win new opportunities. The service-oriented team is now in position to become a self-sustaining team.

Again, I need to reiterate these profiles are based on natural behaviors. The experience/skills of the individual members will play a major role on the ultimate success of the team. If the individuals on the team are positioned with roles and responsibilities that match their natural behaviors, the chances for success are far greater than if not.

THE SELF-SUSTAINING TEAM—THE EVOLUTION

In the previous profile I introduced the difference between a service-oriented team and a self-sustaining team. That profile showed how one simple, yet defined, addition significantly changed the team composition. In this final profile we will examine the evolution of a dynamic, independent, investment team. This Northeast based team focuses on retail and office investment properties and represents half their clients in their local market and the rest in the eastern half of the country.

Over the years the team has grown, has made some hiring mistakes, which we will examine, and has corrected. We will review these stages and you should be able, at this point, to put it all together yourself. This is exactly what I want. I want you to understand how to create your own dominant team and then go out and do it!

The early stages of the team started out like most teams: Two or more producers have an idea of creating a team, maybe breaking away from a national company and feeling they can do it better; they want to be their own boss. This is how this team started. Initially the team consisted of a senior team leader, a senior peer and a mid-career associate. Their initial team profile is displayed as follows:

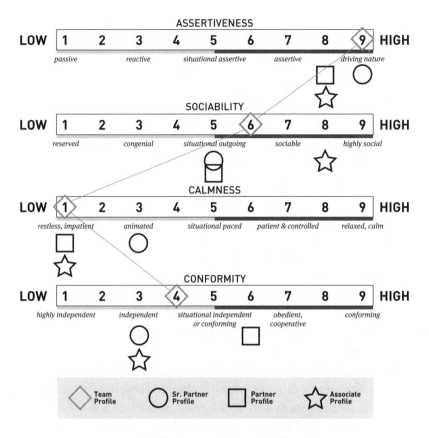

ASSERTIVENESS

LOW	1	2	3	4	5	6	7	8	9	HIGH

passive   *reactive*   *situational assertive*   *assertive*   *driving nature*

SOCIABILITY

LOW	1	2	3	4	5	6	7	8	9	HIGH

reserved   *congenial*   *situational outgoing*   *sociable*   *highly social*

CALMNESS

LOW	1	2	3	4	5	6	7	8	9	HIGH

restless, impatient   *animated*   *situational paced*   *patient & controlled*   *relaxed, calm*

CONFORMITY

LOW	1	2	3	4	5	6	7	8	9	HIGH

highly independent   *independent*   *situational independent or conforming*   *obedient, cooperative*   *conforming*

◇ Team Profile   ◯ Sr. Partner Profile   ☐ Partner Profile   ☆ Associate Profile

Team profile for a self-sustaining team,
before hiring additional personnel

The team pattern is **9-6-1-4**. This pattern suggests that this team is assertive, situationally social, most likely fast paced, very responsive and situationally structured and conforming. Remember, the team pattern is based on a composite of the natural behaviors of the individual members.

The good news is that this non-leader partner (represented by a square) understands her role and is best positioned as a fulfiller of the business. Yes, she tends to be assertive and not very calm, but she is generally structured and this initially afforded the team ability to service the accounts they procured. From her profile **(8-5-1-6)**, we can be confident she knows what she's supposed to do, knows how to do it, and it's happening the way it's supposed to be done and there's no failure. She tends to move fast for her clients too. She can talk to people easily. By nature, generally she is someone who is going to be expeditious but at the same time try to make sure things are being done correctly.

The senior leader partner (represented by a circle, 9-5-3-3) and mid-career associate (represented by a star, 8-8-1-3) provided the team with the horsepower to find and win business. However, the team realized it was capped. Sure, it could find and win business, but they had a limited capacity to service the business they were bringing on. Like many dominant teams, they knew that to expand their business they would need to expand their team. You see, the senior-leader partner (9-5-3-3) is generally decisive and results-oriented. He knows what he wants and is going to make certain he gets it.

Their needs were obvious. With an overwhelming capacity and talent to secure new business, they needed an individual who would be more "behind the scenes"; someone who could not only assist the senior partner with her fulfillment responsibilities but take on fulfillment responsibilities personally.

Again, through a comprehensive recruitment and screening process, the team retained such a person. This new admin completed the AVA, which resulted in a behavior pattern of 3-4-4-9. This is represented by the triangle on the following revised team chart. She tends to be very conservative, moderately to less social, moderately calm and very structured; a very good fit for the administrative position and personality match for this team.

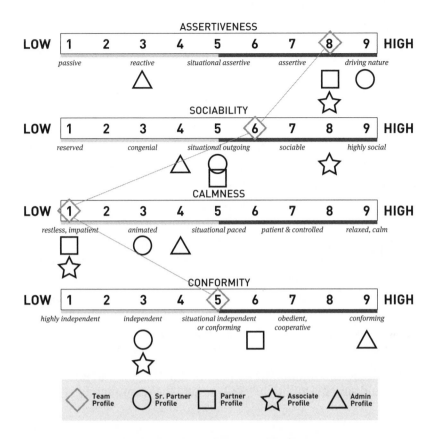

ASSERTIVENESS

LOW	1	2	3	4	5	6	7	8	9	HIGH

| passive | reactive | situational assertive | assertive | driving nature |

SOCIABILITY

LOW	1	2	3	4	5	6	7	8	9	HIGH

| reserved | congenial | situational outgoing | sociable | highly social |

CALMNESS

LOW	1	2	3	4	5	6	7	8	9	HIGH

| restless, impatient | animated | situational paced | patient & controlled | relaxed, calm |

CONFORMITY

LOW	1	2	3	4	5	6	7	8	9	HIGH

| highly independent | independent | situational independent or conforming | obedient, cooperative | conforming |

◇ Team Profile   ◯ Sr. Partner Profile   ▢ Partner Profile   ☆ Associate Profile   △ Admin Profile

***Team profile for a self-sustaining team,
after hiring an administrative assistant***

The revised team composite pattern was **8-6-1-5**. The only variables that shifted with this new addition were that the assertiveness vector moved from 9 to 8 and conformity moved from 4 to 5. The addition of the administrator allowed the team to service additional business as targeted. More importantly, as the administrator became more experienced, it allowed the team to handle high-quality transactions. The team had enhanced their position as self-sustaining team.

The team was now handling more business than before, and the decision was made to add to the team, specifically, to hire another individual to find leasing opportunities to complement the team's already strong investment practice. This time the team decided to hire based on gut feel, versus the previously more comprehensive approach. They found a gentlemen who had the experience in sales outside of commercial real estate and brought him on board.

Unfortunately, this person did not work out as planned. As he experienced more of the requirements of the role and responsibilities of the business development position, he became more uncomfortable and the senior leader, more disenchanted. In retrospect, the problem was obvious. This new prospector was put in a position where he was not naturally comfortable. The emotional energy to prospect for new business was too much to perform at a high level and do so consistently. Upon application of the AVA, we found this new hire had a profile of **3-5-3-9**. Thus he is generally not assertive, yet tends to be more structured—hardly the ideal profile for a new business developer responsible for finding business.

As the following chart shows, the addition of this new ill-positioned "prospector" represented poetically by the "Pacman" symbol, adjusted the team composite profile to **7-6-1-6**, more reflective of a service-oriented perspective than a prospecting perspective. That was not the objective when adding to this team. You could say this addition "gobbled up" the team's momentum!

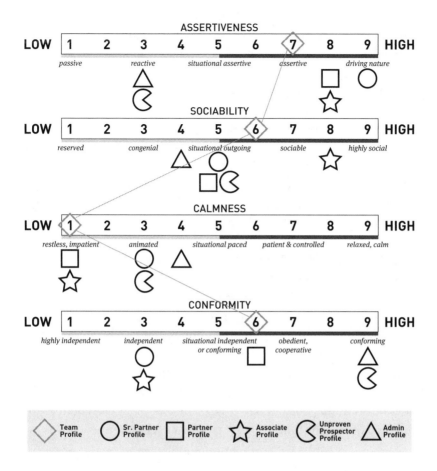

ASSERTIVENESS

LOW	1	2	3	4	5	6	7	8	9	HIGH

passive — *reactive* — *situational assertive* — *assertive* — *driving nature*

SOCIABILITY

LOW	1	2	3	4	5	6	7	8	9	HIGH

reserved — *congenial* — *situational outgoing* — *sociable* — *highly social*

CALMNESS

LOW	1	2	3	4	5	6	7	8	9	HIGH

restless, impatient — *animated* — *situational paced* — *patient & controlled* — *relaxed, calm*

CONFORMITY

LOW	1	2	3	4	5	6	7	8	9	HIGH

highly independent — *independent* — *situational independent or conforming* — *obedient, cooperative* — *conforming*

◇ Team Profile ◯ Sr. Partner Profile ▢ Partner Profile ☆ Associate Profile ℂ Unproven Prospector Profile △ Admin Profile

Team profile for a self-sustaining team, after hiring an unproven prospector

The problem is that this new hire not only lacked the natural behaviors to excel in the position and its associated responsibilities, but he did not have the experience to leverage this mismatch. On top of that, the senior leader partner was expecting a flurry of new business to come from this new hire. It was never going to happen. This was a mismatch from the start.

The team has since decided to return to the size it was, with the two senior partners, the mid-career associate and the administrator/support person. This is the **8-6-1-5** team profile displayed as the second phase. They continue to flourish in investment sales and service not only a greater number of opportunities but a higher quality of opportunities. They are a self-sustaining team. A team built to dominate.

THE IDEAL TEAM—A TEAM BUILT TO DOMINATE

You have now seen profiles for five teams of various sizes, focus points and environments. In addition to these teams, in our consulting practice at the Massimo Group we have analyzed scores of other teams: independent teams, national companies, external teams and internal teams. We have worked with commercial real estate brokers, property management, consulting and mortgage broker/banker teams. So the question you must be asking by now is: "Is there any such thing as an ideal team?

As we attempted to demonstrate to you, the idea of an "ideal team" is based on the environment and the purpose of the team. In a corporate structure or account-based structure, the ideal team will be more service-oriented. However, for a true self-sustaining team, the team must be able to find, win and fulfill the business with equal competency.

Does our research support this? Let's look at various composite patterns of the teams we profiled in this chapter. Yes, the specific team profiles varied, yet they are clustered. Taking into account the teams we profiled in this book, along with the teams we worked with at the Massimo Group, the range of team profiles are clustered as follows:

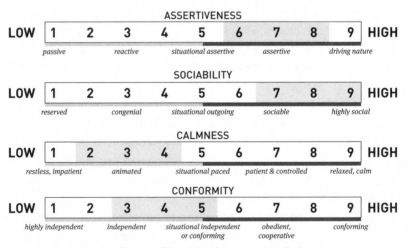

***Composite profile showing range of clusters
for teams profiled by the Massimo Group***

Consistent with our earlier reflection on productive teams, these dominant teams are generally highly assertive and highly social. Furthermore, dominant, self-sustaining teams tend to have a profile reflecting that they are situationally calm; that is, they are very flexible and can adjust, and they are situationally structured and conforming.

If there were an ideal self-sustaining team that is built to dominate, the suggested profile would be **7-8-3-4**, as shown on the following chart.

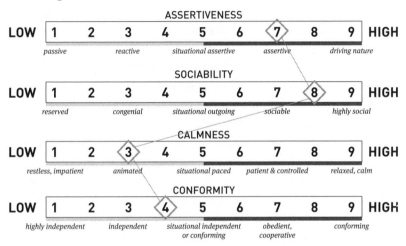

Suggested Profile of the ideal self-sustaining team built to dominate

But wait a minute: that totals 22—more than the defined parameters of the AVA, where the total of all four vectors is always 20! Yes, and Ralph and Dave would quickly remind me that a total of 22 is not possible within the framework of this tool. Actually, it's not possible for an individual, which is why I contend that 20 is not enough.

Individuals will be extremely challenged in today's commercial real estate environment if they try to go it alone. A dominant team needs to be naturally adept at all four vectors, or at least have the flexibility to adapt as necessary.

The AVA is used in this case to support the fact that self-staining teams need to be flexible and possess the abilities to change behaviors in situations where they need to. This in itself cannot be done by an individual, at least not consistently and easily.

From a pure natural behavior perspective:

- **Teams built to dominate are assertive.** They take charge and are relentless in finding new business opportunities. They are not hesitant to ask for those opportunities.
- **Teams built to dominate are social.** Internally, they have an attractive culture, they are fun to be around and fun to work with. Prospects find their nature appealing, and clients remain engaged because the team is likeable.
- **Teams built to dominate are fast paced;** they are agile and deadline oriented. They are adaptable to the demands of the client and are able to provide the level of consistency that is required of them.
- **Teams built to dominate are situationally structured and conforming.** They are able to provide their clients the level of detail and attention they demand to successfully fulfill the clients' business needs. Their cooperative and collaborative approach provides clients with the confidence that they can rely on the team for future opportunities.

Just like with the individual top producers, this "ideal profile" is not set in stone. There are always exceptions. For example, the first team we wrote about has an AVA profile of **4-9-3-4**, and they are one of the most productive (in regards to commissions earned) teams in the country! Yes they are focused on servicing significant accounts, and are more service-oriented, but they are certainly self-sustaining.

As we outlined in this book, dominant teams are not only built on "the right people." Strong leadership, the right structure, effective communication systems and a consistent, appealing culture all have significant impact on molding a team that will attain and maintain their market dominance.

As an individual you can't get there. You can't pursue, procure and service a high number of high-quality clients without a team. Your team may be you and a full-time assistant. Your team may be you and a partner, or a junior. Every team starts somewhere. More importantly, you need the right team—one with defined roles and responsibilities that is positioned for the environment in which the team exists. Beyond the science of natural behaviors, you must balance the individual team member's goals, experience, knowledge and skills.

After reading this chapter, you should now have a better understanding of the science behind constructing a successful team. Now it's time to take all the lessons shared in this book and build or enhance your own dominant team. I know you can. Good luck.

———————•———————

For more information on building your own dominant team, contact us at **www.massimo-group.com/contact**

———————•———————

A VERY SHORT READING LIST ON TEAMS

Originally, I wanted to share a comprehensive reading list about teaming. Unfortunately, good books turned out to be hard to find.

Many popular books were too shallow. They made bold statements but didn't offer any support for them. At the other end of the spectrum were several academic tomes that were too, well, academic and jargon filled. It was very hard to tease out the important stuff, and I thought it would take too long for most people.

Here is a list that consists of two books. They both are well-written, with a lot of good information. For each I'll give you a brief review and a quote from the book.

The Five Dysfunctions of a Team: A Leadership Fable
by Patrick Lencioni

My take: This is one of the most popular books on teams for a good reason. It makes good points and it's easy to read. If business "fables" aren't your thing, just skip right to the section on "The Model." It has a lot of specifics, resources and references.

Beware of one thing with this book. The way the material is presented may lead you to think that the model is linear and that you have to first establish trust, then move on to "Fear of Conflict" and so on through the five dysfunctions. My research says that as most teams develop, all of the dysfunctions are issues. They don't come in any particular order, they do affect each other and you will revisit each one several times.

Here's a quote from *The Five Dysfunctions of a Team*:

In the course of my experience working with CEOs and their teams, two critical truths have become clear to me. First, genuine teamwork in most organizations remains as elusive as it has ever been. Second, organizations fail to achieve teamwork because they unknowingly fall prey to five natural but dangerous pitfalls, which I call the five dysfunctions of a team. These dysfunctions can be mistakenly interpreted as five distinct issues that can be addressed in isolation of the others. But in reality they form an interrelated model, making susceptibility to even one of them potentially lethal for the success of a team.

The Wisdom of Teams:
Creating the High-Performance Organization
by Jon Katzenbach and Douglas Smith

My take: The big upside to this book is solid research and keen observations. The downside is that a lot of the book will not seem relevant to many commercial real estate professionals because it deals with teams in large organizations. I suggest you use the "Look Inside the Book" feature when you check out the book online. The section titled A Note on What to Expect will present you with "Commonsense Findings" and "Uncommonsense Findings." That should give you an idea of whether you want to buy the book. This book was published in 1993, so there is no mention of virtual teams, remote workers, the net, etc.

Here's a quote from *The Wisdom of Teams*:

Team basics include size, purpose, goals, skills, approach and accountability. Paying rigorous attention to these is what creates the conditions necessary for team performance. A deficiency in any of these basics will derail the team, yet most potential teams inadvertently ignore one or more of them.

ABOUT THE AUTHOR

Rod N. Santomassimo is the founder and president of the Massimo Group, the premier commercial real estate consulting and coaching organization in North America. The Massimo Group is proud to include every national commercial real estate firm and scores of regional and local firms and/or their individual professionals among its clients.

Rod Santomassimo has been a featured speaker at a variety of local offices, regional conferences and national conferences, both in and aside from the commercial real estate industry. In addition he has been approved and selected as a featured speaker by the National Association of Realtors Commercial Alliance and its Signature Series.

Rod earned a Master's of Business Administration from Fuqua School of Business, Duke University, in Durham, North Carolina, earned a Bachelor of Arts in Commerce from Washington and Lee University in Lexington, Virginia, and is a featured guest lecturer at the Fuqua School of Business.

Rod is a two-time recipient of the Duke University, Fuqua School of Business Impact Alumni of the Year Award based on his work with both graduate students and alumni in Building a Personal Brand and Creative Approaches to Secure Greater Client/Prospect Opportunities.

Rod's first book, *Brokers Who Dominate—8 traits of top producers*, is an Amazon.com bestseller in commercial real estate brokerage. For more information visit **www.brokerswhodominate.com**

Rod lives in Cary, North Carolina with his wife Launa and their two children.

FOR MORE INFORMATION ON
THE MASSIMO GROUP SERVICES

COACHING

The Massimo Group has the People, Process, and Platforms—as endorsed by your industry peers—to propel you and/or, your team's commercial real estate business to new heights. It is critical, in any coaching relationship, that you align yourself with someone who truly understands your business. The Massimo Group offers both group and 1-to-1 coaching programs for all levels of experience and expertise.

Our market-tested curriculum revisits best practices while introducing new techniques that will have an immediate impact on your and, if applicable, your team's production. Our clients consistently out-earn their industry peers by 4x!

By meeting face-to-face with your coach, via our video conference platform, together you will dissect your current practices and establish a personal plan for maximum production.

———————•———————

To learn more about how we work with our coaching clients, please visit **www.massimo-group.com/coaching**

———————•———————

CONSULTING

There are proven practices and approaches for running a productive organization or team. With over 250 years of combined experience in a wide range of sectors, we can assist you with identifying and implementing our customized solutions, aligned with your vision of success. Owners and team leaders have engaged us for a variety of reasons:

- Recruitment, hiring, and management of top producers
- Working directly with team members to achieve greater personal production
- Staff restructuring to enhance operations efficiency
- Personal time management, organization, and delegation approaches
- Evaluation of new service lines to diversity revenue channels
- Creation and/or evaluation of succession and/or acquisition strategies

To learn how, together, we can provide more effective approaches to managing your growth and maximizing the value of your team, office or organization, please visit **www.massimo-group.com/consulting**

SPEAKING

You need to provide presentations that will attract strong attendance and participation, as well as provide valuable and applicable practices and approaches for finding, winning and fulfilling business. Our presentations, whether for your local office or regional and national conferences, will captivate, motivate and educate. Most importantly, attendees will leave with tangible ideas and defined applications that will have an immediate impact on their business.

To learn more about our speaking programs
and to discuss your presentation needs, please visit
www.massimo-group.com/speaking

BOOKS

Rod's first book, Commercial Real Estate Brokers Who Dominate—8 traits of top producers, quickly became a bestseller on Amazon.com's commercial real estate book list. It continues to be a top-seller. This book explores the 8 key traits necessary to attain and maintain a dominant position as an individual producer. Remember, every dominant team needs a strong producer!

For more information, please visit
www.brokerswhodominate.com

RESOURCES

We offer many free resources on our website, including additional downloads, links to upcoming events, additional products and a free library of Massimo Group, and Massimo Group clients' industry-based publications.

To explore and benefit from our resources, please visit
www.massimo-group.com/resources

Thank you for your investment in time in reading this book. Now it's time for you to create your own Dominant Team.

Keep moving forward.